WHAT'S IN THE BAG

On the cover: A well-dressed and diverse gallery was behind John Boyd Thacher II, Albany's mayor in the 1930s. (Photo courtesy of Mike Daniels)

Copyright 1998 Douglas A. Lonnstrom
All rights reserved.
Published by CML Press, 6154 Veeder Road, Slingerlands, NY 12159
Printed by Lane Press of Albany, Inc.
ISBN 0-9668472-0-2
Library of Congress Catalog Card Number: 98-89169

DEDICATION

TO MY WIFE, Cristine, a great person, a great wife, a great friend, a great golf partner. Without Cris's help and encouragement this book would still be on the practice tee.

THE COURSES: FROM "A" TO "W"

WHEN THEY FIRST TEED IT UP

1.	Otsego Golf Club	1894
2.	Van Schaick Island Country Club	1895
3.	Albany Country Club	1896
4.	Saratoga Golf And Polo Club	1896
5.	Taconic Golf Club	1896
6.	Sacandaga Golf Club	1898
7.	Mohawk Golf Club	1899
8.	Antlers Country Club	1900
9.	Edison Club	1904
10.	Leatherstocking Golf Course	1909
11.	Hoosick Falls Country Club	1910
12.	Mechanicville Golf Club	1910
13.	Colonie Country Club	1913
14.	Glens Falls Country Club	1914
15.	Wolferts Roost Country Club	1915
16.	Columbia Golf And Country Club	1920
17.	Rip Van Winkle Country Club	1920
18.	McGregor Links Country Club	1921
19.	Pine Brook Golf Club	1923
20.	Battenkill Country Club	1925
21.	Burden Lake Country Club	1925
22.	Nick Stoner Municipal Golf Club	1925
23.	Ballston Spa Country Club	1926
24.	Bend Of The River Golf Club	1926
25.	Catskill Golf Club	1927
26.	Country Club Of Troy	1927
27.	Normanside Country Club	1927
28.	Schuyler Meadows Club	1927
29.	Cranwell Resort And Golf Club	1928
30.	Windham Country Club	1928
31.	Cobleskill Golf And Country Club	1929
32.	Sagamore Resort And Golf Club	1929
33.	Shaker Ridge Country Club	1929
34.	Colonial Country Club	1930
35.	Cronin's Golf Resort	1930
36.	Frear Park Golf Course	1931
37.	Kingsboro Golf Club	1931
38.	New Course At Albany	1932
39.	Western Turnpike Golf Course	1932
40.	Schenectady Municipal Golf Course	1935
41.	Amsterdam Municipal Golf Course	1938
42.	Canajoharie Country Club	1939
43.	Top Of The World Golf Resort	1939
44.	Bay Meadows Golf Club	1953

45.	Queensbury Country Club	1955
46.	Rainbow Golf Club	1956
47.	Stadium Golf Club	1957
48.	Pinehaven Country Club	1959
49.	Sunnyside Golf Course	1959
50.	Hiawatha Trails Golf Course	1960
51.	Briar Creek Golf Club	1961
52.	Hillcrest Golf And Country Club	1961
53.	Holland Meadows Golf Course	1962
54.	Pheasant Hollow Golf Club	1962
55.	Tee-Bird Country Club	1962
56.	Winding Brook Country Club	1962
57.	Brookhaven Golf Club	1963
58.	Dutchaven Golf Course	1963
59.	Evergreen Country Club	1963
60.	Saratoga Spa Golf Course	1963
61.	Clifton Knolls Golf Club	1964
62.	Colonial Acres Golf Course	1964
63.	Saratoga Spa Executive Course	1964
64.	Christman's Windham House	1965
65.	Eagle Crest Golf Club	1965
66.	Meadowgreens Golf Club	1965
67.	Whispering Pines Golf Club	1965
68.	Riverview Country Club	1966
69.	Galway Golf Course	1967
70.	Skene Valley Country Club	1967
71.	Sunny Hill Resort And Golf Course	1968
72.	Pleasantview Golf Club	1969
73.	Town Of Colonie Golf Course	1969
74.	Van Patten Golf Course	1969
75.	French's Hollow Fairways	1971
76.	Sycamore Country Club	1971
77.	Thousand Acres Golf Club	1971
78.	Mill Road Acres Golf Course	1974
79.	Wedgewood Golf Club	1974
80.	Duffer's Den	1975
81.	Alban Hills Golf Club	1980
82.	Hiland Golf Club	1988
83.	Blackhead Mountain Country Club	1990
84.	Kingswood Golf Club	1991
85.	MaRia Mountain Golf Course	1992
86.	Tee-Bird South Course	1993
87.	Brunswick Greens Golf Course	1994
88.	Pioneer Hills Golf Club	1995
89.	Windy Hills Golf Course	1995

ALIVE AND WELL:

The Ten Oldest Courses Still at Their Original Sites

1.	Otsego Golf Club	1894
2.	Van Schaick Island Country Club	1895
3.	Saratoga Golf And Polo Club	1896
4.	Taconic Golf Club	1896
5.	Sacandaga Golf Club	1898
6.	Antlers Country Club	1900
7.	Leatherstocking Golf Course	1909
8.	Hoosick Falls Country Club	1910
9.	Mechanicville Golf Club	1910
10.	Glens Falls Country Club	1914

DOWN THE MIDDLE

HEN I STARTED THIS PROJECT in 1995, I was filled with great expectations. Now it is finished, and I'm happy with the results: A book that will provide interesting information and anecdotes for the Capital Region golfer. My research efforts have caused many clubs to write or update their own histories; I hope more will follow. In the process of creating this book, I've learned a great deal:

- Schuyler Meadows was started because the golfers of Loudonville felt Albany Country Club (then located where the University at Albany campus is today) was too far away.

- Shaker Ridge was founded because Slavic Jews were denied membership in Colonie Country Club, which was controlled by German Jews.

- The Schenectady Curling Club exists because Mohawk Golf Club had a fire.

- Lionel F. Callaway, the pro who invented the Callaway Handicap System, worked in the Capital Region as the pro at Sacandaga Golf Club in 1942.

- Karsten Solheim, the creator of Ping, was a General Electric engineer and a member of the Edison Club.

- Gene Sarazen belonged to the Columbia Country Club and played many courses in the Capital Region.

- Fires in the early part of the century played a major role in the history of many local clubs when big, old, wooden clubhouses burned down.

I have been working on this book for more than three years, so there are many people to thank. Special thanks go to three people: Bob Smith, my editor, whose talent and effort have improved this book immensely, Heather

Legendziewicz, whose patience and computer skills saved me from a fourth year of work and Dave Smith, whose ideas and support helped to bring this book to fruition. The following people have also contributed to making this a better book:

David Barrell	Tom Kelly
Bill Berglas	Sean Maloney
Tim Burke	Rene Molineaux
Bonnie Clark	Dave Morris
Harry Clark	Charlie Murphy
Mike Daniels	Larry Packard
Fred DeCasperis	Bob Provost
Lou DeMaria	Gene Sarazen
Gary Denn	Dan Spooner
Janis Dorgan	David Rice
Bill Evans	Ron Stewart
Earl Feiden	Roy Stratton
Dan Gyoerkoe	Ed Unser

Two organizations also provided much support and assistance: Siena College and the USGA.

HAZARDS

I APPROACHED THIS PROJECT with exhilaration, optimism and the desire to make this a comprehensive volume. There were, however, frustrations. Getting complete information from the clubs was difficult. People who run golf courses are very busy. In some cases it took numerous follow-ups, sometimes as many as 10, to obtain a club history. In addition, I researched local newspapers, magazines and books to find other material. In some cases I contacted city and town historians to verify information. I also talked at great length with local golf writers and historians.

I found a great deal of national golf history, but little locally. Area newspapers of the 1880s and 1890s did not have much to offer regarding the origins of golf in the Capital Region. Some articles dealt with matches and tournaments, but little on the organization of clubs.

I need your help. (I need all the help I can get to get out of Hazards). Information on club histories usually came from the club, and there may be errors. Where I had access to a club's original records, I found, for instance: One club with three different dates for its incorporation. Another club's publications with different years for a member winning three State Championships. There are omissions, also. Written histories ranged from none to that of the Mohawk Golf Club. For Mohawk's 75th anniversary, the Club produced a 70-page booklet; for their 100th, a hard cover book. In 1938 they made a film of their history, *Lest We Forget*. What foresight!

Because of the hazards I encountered and constant changes taking place (new history being made), I see a need for a second edition of this book. That's where you come in.

1. Review the history of clubs you know. If you find an error or an omission or know of significant facts, events or interesting stories, please inform me at the address below. Documentation is important.

2. I would like to include a chapter about courses that no longer exist. This is difficult information to obtain, but I think it would bring back fond memories for many of us.

3. I would also like to include a chapter about local golf writers. I have some information, but I need a great deal more.

4. I would like to include more old photos. I have some, but I would love to borrow more from you.

5. I'll be glad to receive any ideas or suggestions that will make the next edition better.

If you have any information or suggestions, please contact me:

Douglas A. Lonnstrom,
100 Lonnstrom Lane
Slingerlands, NY 12159
518-783-2362   518-786-5052 (fax)
E mail: LONNSTROM@SIENA.EDU

Another kind of hazard spotted at French's Hollow

KOLF, COLF OR GOLF COMES TO THE CAPITAL REGION

H OW DID GOLF, as we now know it, get to this region? One of my aims in writing this book was to find the answer to that question. I don't have one. Yet.

I have learned how golf came to our south, east, north and west. John Reid, the "Father of American Golf," was from Yonkers. In 1888, he laid the foundation for the St. Andrews Golf Club and the Apple Tree Gang, so named because the 19th hole was an apple tree. The father of golf to our east is actually a "mother." A wealthy woman from Boston, whose name seems lost in history, saw the game for the first time in France and brought it back to her father's estate. There was organized golf in Canada before it came to the United States. The Royal Montreal Golf Club was established in 1873, 15 years before the Apple Tree Gang. To the west, the Cooperstown area had golf before we did. Wealthy local residents who had been exposed to the game in Florida formed the Otsego Golf Club in 1894.

While I have no definitive answer as to how golf came to the Capital Region, I have some theories.

• Affluent New York City residents who vacationed at the Saratoga Spa or attended the Saratoga Races sparked the development of courses. The fact that the Saratoga Golf and Polo Club (then the Saratoga Golf Club) was founded in 1896 lends support to this idea.

• John C. Ten Eyck, a member of the Apple Tree Gang, may have been a member of the Ten Eyck family, long-time residents of the Capital Region. A member of the local Ten Eyck family, however, does not think their family brought golf here. The New York City Ten Eyck's were a different branch of the family, I am told.

• Since we were surrounded by organized golf, it seeped into our area and there is no one person responsible for bringing it to this area. The Mohawk Golf Club's 75th anniversary booklet refers to member Rudolph Romeling as the "Father of Schenectady Golf," but gives no reason why. In Mohawk's 100th Anniversary book, they dropped this reference.

None of the above. If you have knowledge of any sources that can provide a definitive answer, I hope you will share them with me.

My research leads me to cast serious doubt on the belief that golf was being played here in the 17th century.

Albany (Fort Orange) has received a great deal of publicity for passing a law in 1659 that may have been poorly translated from Dutch to English as: "…against the practice of playing golf along the streets, which causes great damage to the windows of the houses and also exposes people to the danger of being injured…". There is a Dutch game called Kolven that uses a Kolf club, but that is where the resemblance to our game of golf ends. In old histories there is confusion among croquet, hockey, golf and other stick and ball games.

Robert Browning, in his 1955 book, *A History of Golf*, states: "…Kolven is still played in some parts of Holland, and it has little resemblance to golf." H. B. Martin, in his *Fifty Years of American Golf*, writes: "The word kolven appears again two years later in an ordinance of 1659. It is not by any means certain that this actually was golf that they played, since a game called kolven is still played in Holland. It was in the early days played in the churchyard and on the streets, but neither a street nor a churchyard would be a very suitable place for playing anything that resembles modern day golf." Brian Siplo, in his well researched article in "New York Golf 1998," says: "It is the opinion of most experts that the game being played in and around Fort Orange in the 1600s was indeed <u>colf</u>, and that any reference to <u>golf</u> (emphases added) is a misnomer, not to be mistaken for the Scottish golf we know today."

"What's Good for Golf...": The Game and the Economy

As I studied the history of golf locally and nationally, I was struck by the significant impact that the economy has had upon the fortunes of the game. The ups and downs of golf in the Capital Region are directly tied to the ups and downs of the national economy.

Before looking at this region, it is interesting to study the generic origin of country clubs in the United States. In the late 1700s and early 1800s, the rich wanted to escape the city during the summer for two reasons - - the heat and the smell. Many went to spas. (Saratoga was the leading spa in the country around 1800.) Spas, however, were not always in convenient locations. So the rich decided to build resorts in places more convenient for their summer getaways. However, it was not always possible to control the clientele at resorts, and the rich did not want to socialize with people below their station. Hence, the private country club was created, giving the affluent all the amenities they wanted and control of the membership.

Golf in this country and this region exploded during the 1890s, a decade to be known as the "Gay Nineties." It was a happy time, the country was growing, and the Capital Region was booming. General Electric was expanding in Schenectady; state government was growing in Albany. It is no accident that golf also boomed during this decade. In 1888, golfers in the United States numbered in the dozens. By 1900, that number had grown to about 250,000, who spent $20 million a year on the game, a considerable sum in those days. In 1888, there were no golf courses in New York State; by 1900 there were 165. In this area, seven courses got started during the "Gay Nineties."

This growth continued until World War I. The early 1900s were prosperous times. By 1916, there were thousands of courses in the country and 15 in the Capital Region. The war brought a temporary halt to the growth as resources became tighter. Men, money and material were devoted to fighting the war. These circumstances took their toll on golf clubs, but only for a few years.

The "Roaring Twenties," perhaps the greatest boom time in the history of the country, followed the war years. From 1918 until the stock market crash in October 1929, the growth of golf was extraordinary. Eighteen new courses were built in our area during the 1920s. Before the war, clubhouses were modest buildings, often converted farmhouses. During the "Roaring Twenties," opulent, million-dollar clubhouses were built, private clubs abounded and the affluent often built courses on their estates.

The years from 1929 to 1945 are the darkest in the history of golf. The crash of '29 was followed by the Depression of the '30s and America's entry into World War II in 1941. Some courses were built in the Capital Region during the 1930s, but several closed. No new courses were built between 1939 and 1953. Money was tight, members dropped out of private clubs (clubs added assessments to make up for lost members which, of course, drove out more members) and clubs went into debt. Young men went off to fight another war. Writers of the period predicted a gloomy future for golf. Some questioned if the game would even survive.

They were wrong. After World War II, golf boomed again. In the Capital Region, 31 courses were built during the 1950s and 1960s. The "look" of golf changed, too. During the first half of the century men dominated golf. Women were not allowed in certain clubs. In others, they had limited tee times and clubhouse restrictions. After the war, many clubs became more family oriented. Women and juniors started to play in greater numbers. Swimming pools and other non-golf activities were added. Family social events were created. The impact of Arnold Palmer, a working class joe from Latrobe, PA, spread golf to the masses and more public courses were built.

The 1970s — with the Vietnam War, Watergate and the 20 percent interest rates of the Jimmy Carter Years — caught up with golf's growth. Many of the Capital Region's prestige clubs lost members for two reasons: Older members were dying off, and the national anti-establishment mood kept many young people from joining. Coupled with high interest rates, clubs started to hurt financially. In the late 1970s and early 1980s, the prestige clubs were trying to attract members from other clubs. They reduced or eliminated initiation fees (which had been in the thousands) and allowed one-year trial memberships. The growth of public courses slowed considerably, also.

The Reagan Years brought golf back. Interest rates came down, the economy grew and it became respectable again to belong to a private club and play golf. The only glitches in recent years were the tax reforms of the late 1980's and early 1990s that limited entertainment expenses in general and prohibited the deduction of club dues. These tax changes hurt many local clubs economically. Some people who had belonged to two clubs cut back to one and memberships dropped. But most clubs have rebounded, and Capital Region golf is in a growth mode. New courses are being built and older courses are either improving their facilities or expanding. All signs are positive on the eve of the 21st century.

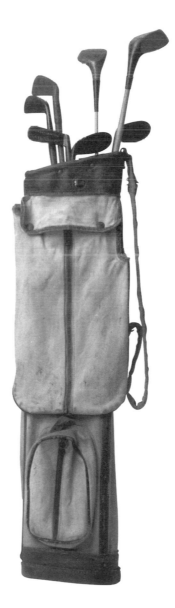

THE VIEW FROM THE WOMEN'S TEES

THE HISTORY OF WOMEN in golf in this country and the Capital Region is a mixed bag. H. B. Martin, in his 1936 classic *Fifty Years of American Golf,* devotes a chapter to women golfers titled "The Feminine Influence." The opening sentence reads, "The feminine interest in the game of golf has been of dominating importance almost from the very beginning." Indeed, Mary, Queen of Scots, played golf in the 1500's. Herbert Warren Wind in *The Story of American Golf* states that by 1900 golf in the United States was a sport that was "... open to both sexes and a wide range of ages...."

As mentioned elsewhere in this book, golf established a strong foothold in this country during the "Gay Nineties." Indeed, women's golf generally got off to a good start. Women introduced golf in Boston and Montclair, NJ in 1892. In 1894, women built and ran their own course in Morristown, NJ. However, the very first American club, St. Andrews, did not have women members or even allow women to play the course. St. Andrews was not alone. These all-men clubs were referred to as "Eveless Edens." In the beginning, the wives of the St. Andrews members were thrilled that their husbands were playing golf: It got them out of the house on weekends and holidays. However, they soon realized that the men were on the course from early spring until late fall. Those wives were the first "golf widows." Their response was to build their own golf course, called Saegkill, a little north of Yonkers. They were among the early American women golfers known as "golferines."

In golf's American beginnings, women were encouraged to play in most places. The reason was simple: There were so few players the courses were not crowded; to succeed financially women were needed. Shinnecock Hills on Long Island was the first club to build a first-class clubhouse. Designed by Frank Lloyd Wright, the fine facility was intended to attract more women and encourage a better social life. In 1891, Shinnecock Hills built a 12-hole course, and women were very active players. By 1893 the course was crowded, and the club built a special nine-hole course for women. (It isn't clear whether this new course was to encourage more women to play or to get them off the main course.)

As golf became more popular, the financial need for women players declined, and restrictions were placed on them regarding tee times and clubhouse access. Men started making up stories to scare women off the courses. Many of the first courses were cut out of pastures, and men would tell tales about dangerous bulls on the course. They also concocted stories about poisonous snakes. They tried to convey the impression that the holes out of sight of the clubhouse were far too dangerous for women. Serious women players were undeterred.

There are numerous pictures of Capital Region women in the 1890s playing golf in tent skirts and frilly blouses, outfits not conducive to good scores. By the 1920s, women were wearing knickers. By the 1930s, the dress was not dissimilar from today — a short skirt and sweater, much better attire for playing golf.

In 1895, the USGA held its first official national championship for men. They did not conduct one for women, so in the fall of that year, women held their own, informal national championship. The following year this situation was corrected, and the first "National Championship for Women" was conducted. The word "Women" was used in the name for an express purpose. In Great Britain, the title was "Ladies." In America, women wanted it made clear that this new championship was one of gender and not gentility. That first national championship had 25 players, including the Oliver sisters, Cora and Elizabeth, members at Albany Country Club. Cora shot 105 and tied for fifth, which qualified her for the match play portion of the tournament. She lost to the eventual runner-up. Elizabeth shot 116 and finished tenth. The Capital Region should be proud of the extraordinary accomplishments of two local women in the first national championship. Two years later, a third sister, Marion, also of Albany Country Club, lost in the semi-finals.

So by 1900 the bag was mixed: Some clubs did not allow women at all. Others allowed women to play and use the clubhouse but on a restricted basis. Others allowed women to use facilities on an equal basis. Still others were organized and run by women. After the turn of the century, however, women golfers found themselves in the deep rough, so to speak. As golf became more popular and the automobile made transportation easier, courses became crowded and more restrictions were placed on women. Some of the courses that were built by women and others that were built for women were taken over by men. Originally, the prestigious Island Club in Garden City, Long Island allowed women to be members. The last one resigned in 1913.

Locally, the situation followed the national trend. This was a time when men went off to work and women stayed at home to raise children. Club members believed it made sense to restrict tee times for women on weekends. This "custom" continued (and in some instances still does) until the 1950s. Several events came together to change things. The Depression of the 1930s was a tough time for clubs. The poor economy reduced membership and crowding on the courses. Since the courses were not crowded, there was little reason for restrictions. In fact, players were needed. In 1934, Kingsboro created a women's Board of Governors to encourage women to join and play. St. Andrews allowed its first women's tournament in 1935. (However, they still did not allow women members). World War II compounded the problem. While the economy was better, there were few young men around to play golf. Some clubs closed or reduced operations. After the war, many clubs became family oriented rather that male dominated. The trauma of separation during the war was a boon to family activities. More women and juniors starting learning and playing golf. Clubs provided instruction for women and children. Swimming pools, tennis courts and other non-golf activities were added, contributing to an expanded social life.

Into that atmosphere came an odd couple that took golf to a new level in this country: Arnold Palmer and President Dwight Eisenhower. The charismatic, down-to-earth manner of Palmer and the frequent pictures of "Ike" on the course almost overnight took golf from being a sport of the favored rich to a game that reached the middle classes. Not long after, women began working outside the home in increasing numbers. Weekend restrictions of tee times were anathema to them. As the women's movement gained strength, many women saw such discrimination as simply wrong. As a result, more public courses were built by public agencies and by private developers who saw a moneymaking opportunity. These public courses did not have any restrictions on women and often had events in which men and women competed with each other.

In the Capital Region, only a few private clubs were created during this time. Pinehaven Country Club, formed in 1959, is the last private club to be built – and to remain private – in this area. A new development occurred during the 1970s and '80s: The building or major upgrading of upscale resorts. Three from our region that fit this description are Cranwell in Lenox, Leatherstocking in Cooperstown and Sagamore in Lake George. These courses cater to tourists as well as local golfers and have no restrictions on women.

Golf continues to boom and discrimination against women continues to decline. Some private clubs retain certain restrictions but, in many cases, they are being eased. Rooms that were for men only are now open to women, tee time restrictions are less severe, women are getting more and equal tournaments, they are competing in what were men-only events and more events are open to men and women. In 1992, Colonie Country Club, one of the prestige private clubs, removed the restriction on tee times for women.

A final note: In 1928, women golfers in London were accused of being "unsportsmanlike and discourteous" on the links. One of the charges was that they teed off before the group in front had hit their second shots. On Sept. 1, 1928, the Albany Times Union published an interview with leading local women golfers who stated that such things did not happen here. The women interviewed (with photos) were Mrs. W. W. Cadby, Mrs. J. A. Manning (wife of the club president), and Mrs. George Lawyer, all from Schuyler Meadows. Also Mrs. J. E. Heslin and Mrs. Fred J. Stephens from Albany Country Club, Mrs. William E. Walsh from Wolferts Roost, Mrs. Nellie McMasters from Mohawk Country Club and Christina Stevens from the Hoosick Falls Country Club.

THE BUILDERS: NATIONAL ARCHITECTS
WHO DESIGNED LOCAL COURSES

So You Want To Build A Golf Course

By Larry Packard*,
Golf Course Architect

WHAT MAKES A GREAT golf course?

The first consideration is the useable land area - 150 to 160 acres for 18 holes. Golf is played on land, not water, a fact often overlooked in Florida where many courses have water in play on almost every hole!

The course should be at least 7000 yards long from the back tees to accommodate tournament play. Gently rolling land is ideal for a golf course. Some trees, open land and a little water in the form of brooks or small ponds make a perfect setting.

The holes should all be of different lengths, thus requiring the use of every club in the bag. The holes should run clockwise around the property, and there should be no holes where the player is shooting east in the morning or west in the afternoon.

Fifty or 60 sand traps are needed on a first-class course. The greens should have a putting area of between 5000 and 8000 square feet. A green smaller than 5000 square feet is too hard to maintain with normal play. A green larger than 8000 square feet will be wasteful of putting area. Fairways should average 40 yards in width. Some of the holes should be dogleg or double doglegs to create greater playability. There should be five teeing areas to allow for at least two options for the shortest hitters and three for the longer ones.

There are four essentials for a great golf course:

1. Adequate suitable land
2. The best affordable architect
3. The best affordable golf course builders
4. An experienced golf course superintendent and crew for excellent maintenance.

Any golf course built to these standards will be a fine layout.

---

* Larry Packard of Tarpon Springs, FL and Milbrook, NY learned the basics of golf course architecture at Massachusetts State College. After seven years apprenticeship with golf architect Robert Harris, he formed his own design firm, Packard & Wadsworth. Four years later, Larry headed the design firm of Packard, Inc. He has designed or re-designed more than 300 golf courses around the world. His designs includes the 72-hole complex at Innisbrook G&C, considered by many to be his finest work and recognized for years as one of golf *Golf Digest's* Top 100 courses. He is renowned for his environmental concerns and was an early advocate of the use of waste water for course irrigation.

Ten golf course architects with national and international reputations have designed more than two dozen of the courses in the Capital Region. The big names who've turned fields into fairways include Devereux Emmet, Robert Trent Jones, William F. Mitchell, Donald James Ross, Albert W. Tillinghast and William H. Tucker.

Emmet had the greatest impact of any golf architect on the Capital Region. Between 1896 and 1926, he designed eight local courses:

Albany Country Club (the original course);

Edison Club;

Leatherstocking Golf Course;

McGregor Links Country Club;

Mechanicville Golf Club;

Mohawk Golf Club;

Schenectady Country Club (which no longer exists);

Schuyler Meadows Club.

Emmet made his reputation when he designed the Island Club, now the Garden City Golf Club on Long Island, in 1897. He gave the members an excellent course at a low price – and a course that would grow grass, a feat in his day. He went on to design more than 50 courses in New York and some 30 more in 10 other states. Perhaps his most famous course is Congressional Country Club, site of the U.S. Open in 1964 and 1997.

In 1996, the local clubs at courses he designed created the annual Devereux Emmet Tournament. David Morris, a member of McGregor and a former member of Schuyler Meadows, initiated the idea. McGregor hosted and won the first match; Leatherstocking followed suit in 1997. Mechanicville prevailed in 1998. The Emmet Cup, donated by Morris, Jim Carroll of Schuyler Meadows and Bill Willig of Mohawk, is held by the winning club for a year.

Jones, who designed nearly 500 course throughout the world, is golf's most significant architect. In the Capital Region, he designed four courses:

Albany Country Club's present course;

Amsterdam Municipal Golf Course;

Frear Park Golf Course's second nine;

Town of Colonie Golf Course's third nine.

Born in England but educated in the United States and at Cornell University, Jones is noted for his long tee boxes and big greens. His philosophy was that a hole should be a hard par but an easy bogey. His son, Rees, renovated the Congressional Course before the 1997 Open.

Mitchell had an excellent background for a golf course architect. He was the son of an agricultural teacher and golf superintendent. He designed more than 150 new courses and redesigned another 200. Locally, he is responsible for five courses:

> Pheasant Hollow Golf Club;
> Riverview Country Club;
> Saratoga Spa Executive Course;
> Saratoga Spa Golf Course;
> Town of Colonie Golf Course's first 18 holes.

A supporter of golf courses for women, Mitchell was employed by the LPGA. He is credited with creating the term "executive course," a combination of par 3s and 4s.

Ross, a native of Scotland, came to the United States in 1899. As greenskeeper at Oakley Country Club in Boston, he met the Tufts family that was developing Pinehurst in North Carolina. His work there made him well known and highly sought after. He designed three courses in the Capital Region:

> Glens Falls Country Club;
> Rip Van Winkle Country Club;
> Sagamore Resort And Golf Club.

He designed and remodeled hundreds of courses in 30 states, Canada, Cuba and Scotland. Ross was noted for using natural terrain, even for his greens, and for emphasizing the short game.

Tillinghast, of the Philadelphia Tillinghasts, was known as "Tillie the Terror." His most notable course designs are at Baltusrol, Bethpage and Winged Foot. In 1921, he redesigned the original nine at Wolferts Roost and designed a second nine. (Harold F. Andrews, an Albany engineer, designed the original nine.) Tillinghast is credited with creating the term "birdie."

Tucker came to the United States from England at the age of 24. A recognized turf expert, he was involved in the design or redesign of more than 100 courses, including the St. Andrews Golf Club in Hastings-on-Hudson in 1898. In this area he designed the Antlers Country Club.

Other national golf architects and their local courses include:

    Geoffrey S. Cornish: Colonie Country Club's present location;

    Stephen Kay: Hiland Golf Club;

    Harold "Hal" Purdy: Columbia Golf and Country Club,
      Sunnyhill Golf Course and Windham Country Club;

    Walter Travis: Country Club of Troy.

As you would expect, local architects figured prominently in the growth of Capital Region courses and golf. Those who designed several courses in the area include:

    Mark Cassidy: Skene Valley Country Club, Queensbury Country Club, Vacationland (now Cronin's Golf Resort);

    Armand Farina: Ballston Spa Country Club, Pinehaven Country Club, Van Patten Golf Course;

    John Melville: Frear Park Golf Course's first nine holes, Albany Municipal Golf Course (now New Course at Albany)

    Jim Thompson: Ballston Spa Country Club, Catskill Golf Club, Colonie Country Club's former location, Pinehaven Country Club, Schenectady Municipal Golf Course, Shaker Ridge Country Club, Western Turnpike Golf Course;

    Gino Turchi: Ballston Spa Country Club, Northway Heights (now Eagle Crest).

ARTHUR KNIGHT AND HIS
SCHENECTADY PUTTER

A RTHUR F. "BILL" KNIGHT, a General Electric engineer at the turn of the century, brought attention to the Electric City, but not through his work with GE. A member of the Mohawk Golf Club and Club Champion in 1900, 1901 and 1902, Knight invented the Schenectady Putter (1899) and developed steel shafts (1908).

The Schenectady Putter was a center shafted, mallet type putter. Knight used it at Mohawk in 1902, the same year he applied for and received a patent. Devereux Emmet, a leading golf course architect and designer of Mohawk, borrowed the Putter and lent it to Walter J. Travis, a leading amateur player famous for trying anything that would help his putting. Travis used the Schenectady Putter in the 1902 US Open and finished second. He won the US Amateur three times before 1904.

In 1904, Travis took the Putter to Sandwich, England and won the British Open at Royal St. Georges. The British were not happy, to say the least. The Royal and Ancient Golf Club of St. Andrews, the British equivalent of the USGA, took up the issue of club design. In 1908, the R&A inserted "...it will not sanction any substantial departure from the traditional and accepted form and make of golf clubs..." in the rules, the first reference to club making.

In 1909, the Nga Motu Golf Club in New Zealand requested a ruling from the R&A regarding use of a croquet mallet as a putter. The R&A denied the request. That same year the Pickeridge Golf Club asked if using "... a putter made in the form of a croquet mallet" was permissible. As a result, of this request the R&A banned all putters "... of the mallet-headed type..." in 1910. The USGA accepted the general rule on mallets, but decided that the Schenectady Putter did not fit the category. The Putter was never banned in the United States, and in 1952 the R&A lifted its sanction against center-shafted putters.

In 1902, Knight formed the Schenectady Putter Company. He sold 500 putters at $2.50 each. He later changed the name to the Schenectady Golfclub Company. A.G. Spalding made the Schenectady Putter popular. He was having trouble getting clubs from Scotland to meet the demand, so he set up his own factory. The Schenectady Putter, known as a "Hammer Headed Putter," had some loft, so a player could also chip with it. A complete club cost $3, but the head alone could be purchased for $2. It was estimated in 1910 that nearly 50 per cent of American golfers were using the Schenectady Putter. By this time, Travis had switched to a different style.

The Schenectady Putter was not the only invention in Knight's bag. In his era, shafts were made of wood. In 1910, Knight developed steel tubing to be used for shafts, and he made both step down and tapered shafts. It was not until 1924 that the USGA permitted metal shafts. The R&A approved of them in 1929.

Knight was also interested in golf course architecture. He worked with Emmet on the design of the Mohawk course. In 1927, he helped Emmet with the design of the Edison Club. In 1935, he worked on the design of the Schenectady Municipal Golf Course. Knight died in 1936, the year that the 15th hole at Mohawk was redesigned using his ideas and named for him. A memorial stone near the tee honors him.

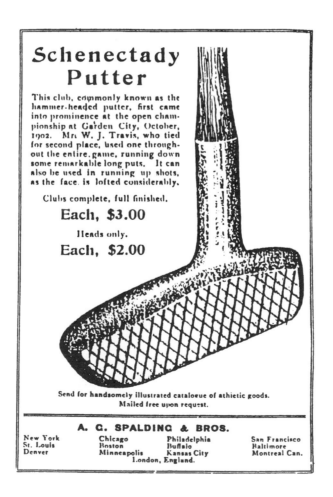

Divots (and Other Loose Items)

Slope And Course Rating

I have included the slope and course rating, where appropriate, for each course in this history. However, I find that the average golfer does not really understand the meaning of these terms. I will try to work through the technical material and give you the general sense of these terms. The following definitions come from "The USGA Handicap System" booklet, effective Jan. 1, 1998.

COURSE RATING indicates "… the playing difficulty of a course for scratch golfers under normal course and weather conditions. … based on yardage and other obstacles to the extent that they affect the scoring ability of a scratch golfer." But what is a scratch golfer? The USGA definition: male "… hit tee shots an average of 250 yards and can reach a 470-yard hole in two shots." female "… hit tee shots an average of 210 yards and can reach a 400-yard hole in two shots."

SLOPE measures "… the relative difficulty of a course for players who are not scratch golfers.…" Slope can be as low as 55 and as high as 155. The USGA uses 113 for a course of average relative difficulty. Courses are not only rated for scratch golfers, but for bogey golfers. "A male bogey golfer has a USGA Handicap Index of 17.5 to 22.4. He can hit tee shots an average of 200 yards and can reach a 370-yard hole in two shots. …A female bogey golfer has a USGA Handicap Index of 21.5 to 26.4. She can hit tee shots an average of 150 yards and can reach a 280-yard hole in two shots."

In summary, we need to combine course and slope ratings. If the difference between scratch and bogey golfers is small, the slope will be low. If the difference is large, the slope will be high. Presumably, the more difficult the course, the more the bogey golfer is penalized relative to the scratch golfer, thus receiving more strokes.

To complete this discussion we need to look at two more terms:

HANDICAP INDEX indicates "… a player's potential scoring ability on a course of standard playing difficulty."

COURSE HANDICAP is "… the number of handicap strokes a player receives from a specific set of tees at the course being played to adjust his scoring ability to the common level of scratch or 0-handicap golf."

Therefore, if you are playing a standard course (slope of 113) your index and handicap should be the same. If the slope of the course you are playing is lower than 113, your handicap allowance that day will go down. If the slope is higher than 113, then your handicap that day will be greater than your index. Rest assured, if you are invited to play Winged Foot, you will get extra strokes.

I love the USGA definition of Par: "Par is the score that an expert golfer would be expected to make for a given hole. Par means errorless play without flukes under ordinary weather conditions, allowing two strokes on the putting green."

Now I don't feel so bad!

Albany National Golf Club: The club without real estate

On Feb. 23, 1995, 16 golfers formed a new golf club, one without a course. They wanted to play first-class golf with friends without all the hassles of a country club: dining room, tennis, pool, clubhouse, etc. The 16 were:

John Aquino	Bill Horan
Kevin Broderick	Eric King
Joe Bonkoski	John Laurent
Kevin Cassidy	John Malfetano
Tom Coyle Jr.	John Mellen
John Davis	Joe Pickett
Gary Denn	Chuck St. Lucia
Jim Hettie	Paul Westfall

By-laws were written, Tom Coyle Jr. was elected president and Gary Denn was elected secretary. The USGA recognizes the concept of a club without a course, and Albany National applied for membership. USGA certification was received on March 2, 1995. Albany National also joined the New York State Golf Association on May 18, 1995.

Annual dues have always been $10, and the Club operates in the black. Four major tournaments are held each year: Tradition, Member-Member, Club Championship and Classic. These are played at top-rated facilities, generally within a two-hour drive of Albany. Winners of the tournaments receive medals in the tradition of the famous clubs of the United Kingdom. Members often play together in less organized outings.

Albany National provides a USGA sanctioned handicap service for its members. The club has its own logo, and members may purchase caps, golf shirts and wind shirts as well as receive bag tags. Membership was 81 the first year, grew to 104 in 1996, 131 in 1997 and in 1998 stands at 109 (as of July 1998).

Eastern New York Golf Association – ENYGA

The Association was founded in 1932 to promote golf on the local level. It was started by the private clubs to give their members the opportunity to play the other private courses. Clubs paid dues to become members of ENYGA. This arrangement continued until the 1960s when some of the clubs decided it was not worth the dues to belong because only a few members were playing in the ENYGA. As the private clubs dropped out, public courses were allowed to join. As a result, more of the private clubs dropped out, and by 1990 there were no member clubs. Players today join as individuals.

Gene Fitzpatrick essentially ran the organization from the 1960s to 1975. Earl Feiden then served eight years as president and implemented many of the changes in use today. Louis DeMaria served as Feiden's treasurer, then six more years as president. Among changes they implemented were starting times, restructuring the prize system and founding the Challenge Cup that pitted the local amateurs against the local pros for bragging rights.

ENYGA involves golfers from Eastern New York, Western Vermont and Massachusetts. Players pay annual dues of $20 to become members; the entry fee for the weekly events is also $20. There are approximately 250 members, and the average number of players per week is 150. Gross and net prizes are awarded in different handicap groups. About 20 tournaments are held each year. There are also special junior and senior tournaments as well as club championships and the Lou Torre team event, named for the local golf writer.

Cliff Hughes has been running the ENYGA Junior Tournaments since 1974. He will retire in 1999 after 25 years of service. Juniors go to age 18 and then can join the regular ENYGA. They receive free dues the first year.

Since 1989, Harry and Bonnie Clark have organized the events. Harry is the tournament director/treasurer and Bonnie is the secretary. The president is Ron Farrigan.

Northeastern New York Section Professional Golfers' Association Of America – NENYPGA

The Professional Golfers' Association of America was formed in New York City in 1916. Rodman Wanamaker, of department store fame, was instrumental in its founding. The winner of the PGA Championship each year receives the Wanamaker Trophy.

The objectives of the PGA were:
- Promote interest in the game of golf.
- Elevate the standards of the golf professional's vocation.
- Protect the mutual interest of its members.
- Hold meetings and tournaments for the benefit of members.
- Assist deserving unemployed members to obtain positions.
- Establish a benevolent relief fund for deserving members.
- Accomplish any other objective which may be determined by the Association from time to time.

Pros from the Capital Region were active from the very beginning and three, Alex McIntyre of Schenectady, Eddie Schultz of Country Club of Troy and Jim Thompson of Mohawk Golf Club, attended the first organizational meeting. Around 1926, this area split from the Metropolitan Section to form the NENYPGA. It thus became the second section in the country.

Currently the NENYPGA has 132 members, all class "A" professionals. Fourteen of these pros serve on the Board of Directors, which determines policy. Jim Hefti of Ballston Spa Country Club is the current president. Dan Gyoerkoe was hired to be executive director in 1995.

The mission of the NENYPGA "... is to promote interest, participation and enjoyment in the game of golf; establish and maintain professional standards; and develop programs to enhance the well being of its members." The objectives are:
1. Establish and encourage a supportive environment among PGA members, including: Organized competition with fellow members and amateurs of all levels, meetings, and benefits.
2. Encourage the use of and employment of PGA professionals by providing services to golfers and the golf industry.
3. Enhance the skill levels of all members and apprentices through education.
4. Provide services to support national programs within the section.

5. Promote enjoyment and participation in the game of golf by providing programs and services to the amateur golfing public.
6. Educate owners and Boards of member and non-member facilities to the benefits of employing a PGA professional.

The association runs an active tournament program for section pros, conducts education seminars for members regarding rules, teaching, management, playing, etc. (each pro must complete 36 hours of continuing education every three years to remain certified) and operates a junior golf program in which more than 700 youngsters participate each year.

Seniors Inter-Club Golf Association

In 1993, Earl Feiden and Louis DeMaria founded the Association. The purpose was "to arrange Inter-Club golf tournaments each year among the Member Clubs." The objectives are to further the advancement of the game of golf, promote good sportsmanship and friendly rivalry among players and to provide an opportunity to make new golfing acquaintances. The member clubs are:

Albany Country Club
Colonie Country Club
Country Club of Troy
Edison Club
Mohawk Golf Club
Normanside Country Club
Pinehaven Country Club
Schuyler Meadows Club
Shaker Ridge Country Club

Feiden served as president for the first two years, and DeMaria is the president now.

Five monthly tournaments are held each year at various clubs.

Teams consist of 11 players from each club, but only the low seven net scores count. There are team and individual prizes at each event, and the low total team for the year wins the Earl B. Feiden Trophy.

Top Ten Courses: From Tee to Green

Top Ten – Slope –Back Tees

		Slope
1.	Hiland Golf Club	133
1.	McGregor Links Country Club	133
3.	Town Of Colonie Golf Course	132
4.	Albany Country Club	131
5.	Evergreen Country Club	131
6.	Sagamore Resort And Golf Club	130
6.	Saratoga Spa Golf Course	130
8.	Schuyler Meadows Club	129
9.	Kingswood Golf Club	128
9.	Riverview Country Club	128
9.	Wolferts Roost Country Club	128

Top Ten – Course Rating –Back Tees

		Rating
1.	Saratoga Spa Golf Course	74.0
2.	Riverview Country Club	73.7
3.	Colonie Country Club	73.6
4.	Evergreen Country Club	73.5
5.	Albany Country Club	73.4
6.	Schuyler Meadows Club	73.2
7.	Sagamore Resort And Golf Course	72.9
8.	Hiland Golf Club	72.5
8.	Town Of Colonie Golf Course	72.5
10.	Eagle Crest Golf Club	72.4

Top Ten – Total Yards –Back Tees

		Yards
1.	Evergreen Country Club	7244
2.	Riverview Country Club	7095
3.	Saratoga Spa Golf Course	7078
4.	Albany Country Club	7051
5.	Colonie Country Club	6981
6.	Town Of Colonie Golf Course	6845
7.	Skene Valley Country Club	6823
8.	Eagle Crest Golf Club	6814
9.	Sagamore Resort And Golf Club	6809
10.	Schuyler Meadows Club	6787

Top Ten – Slope –Front Tees

		Slope
1.	Evergreen Country Club	133
2.	Cranwell Resort And Golf Club	129
3.	Schuyler Meadows Club	127
4.	Albany Country Club	125
4.	Colonie Country Club	125
4.	McGregor Links Country Club	125
4.	Mohawk Golf Club	125
8.	Riverview Country Club	124
9.	Edison Club	123
9.	Hiland Golf Club	123
9.	Shaker Ridge Country Club	123
9.	Taconic Golf Club	123

Top Ten – Course Rating –Front Tees

		Rating
1.	Evergreen Country Club	76.5
2.	Colonie Country Club	74.9
3.	Mohawk Golf Club	73.8
4.	Riverview Country Club	73.4
5.	Country Club Of Troy	73.0
5.	Pinehaven Country Club	73.0
5.	Sagamore Resort And Golf Club	73.0
8.	Hiland Golf Club	72.5
8.	Schuyler Meadows Club	72.5
10.	Cranwell Resort And Golf Club	72.4
10.	Winding Brook Country Club	72.4

Top Ten – Total Yards –Front Tees

		Yards
1.	Colonie Country Club	5986
2.	Pinehaven Country Club	5964
3.	Winding Brook Country Club	5865
4.	Town Of Colonie Golf Course	5810
5.	Cronin's Golf Resort	5757
6.	Mohawk Golf Club	5751
7.	Skene Valley Country Club	5688
8.	Hiland Golf Club	5677
9.	Albany Country Club	5675
10.	Saratoga Spa Golf Course	5611

FACES AND PLACES OF THE PAST

When it comes to parking, not much has changed at Schuyler Meadows Club since the 1920s. (Photo courtesy of Mike Daniels)

The Albany Country Club clubhouse on Western Avenue before the turn of the century. (Photo courtesy of Albany Country Club)

That's John D. Rockefeller posing for the camera at the old Albany Country Club on July 11, 1929. (Photo courtesy of Mike Daniels)

A summer day in 1939 was a fine time for fishing for young Art Satoski at the pond next to the clubhouse at the Western Turnpike Golf Course. Yes, that's the same Art Satoski that is the owner of Western Turnpike today. (Photo courtesy of Western Turnpike)

Gene Sarazen, who has doffed his cap on golf courses around the world, has played many Capital Region courses. (Photo courtesy of Siena College)

Championship tennis was an attraction at Mohawk Country Club on this day in the 1920s, but golfers (upper right) were still about their important business. (Photo courtesy of Mike Daniels)

Colonie Country Club's clubhouse on the corner of Wolf Road and Central Avenue was remodeled and expanded several times between 1915 and 1961, when the site was sold to Sears. (Photo courtesy of Mike Daniels)

Mrs. Monas Rosenthal and Mrs. Julius Perlmutter were ready to play a round at Shaker Ridge Country Club on August 12, 1960. (Photo courtesy of Mike Daniels)

Players, caddies and spectators paid close attention to this putt on the 18th green at Shaker Ridge Country Club in 1935. (Photo courtesy of Mike Daniels)

Back in 1904, a windmill on the north side of the 14th fairway was an odd structure on the Wolferts Roost course. (Photo courtesy of Wolferts Roost Country Club)

Mrs. Van Parshall displayed good golf form but odd attire, especially her footwear, when she posed for this picture at Normanside Country Club. (Photo courtesy of Mike Daniels)

"6th Fairway 195 yards from tee to green" is the cryptic message on the back of this photo taken at Frear Park Golf Course. (Photo courtesy of Mike Daniels)

ALBAN HILLS GOLF CLUB

JOHNSTOWN, NY

Public, 18 holes

	Par	Slope	Rating	Front nine	Back nine	Total
Front tees	70	105	67.6	2335	2759	5094
Back tees	70	103	66.3	2801	3204	6005

CHRONOLOGY

1974   Land is purchased next to the airport.

1979   Construction begins on the course. Attilio "Til" Albanese and Mario M.
Albanese are the founders and developers. Construction starts under the
supervision of Til Albanese who, along with numerous members of both
families, builds the course.

1980   First nine holes open.

1987   Second nine opens. In the fall, the Fulton County Airport takes some of
the land for the runway, and the entire course has to be redesigned. The
course returns temporarily to nine holes.

1990   The redesigned 18-hole course opens.

NOTES

Til started his golf career at Pine Brook under the direction of Warren Gallagher.
In 1952, he served as both the pro and superintendent at Canajoharie Country
Club. In 1953, Til started to build the Crown Point Country Club in Springfield,
VT, where he lived until 1987.

Mario M. Albanese, an attorney and former Fulton County Judge and Surrogate, is
active in golf circles and a well known area amateur golfer.

ALBANY COUNTRY CLUB

VOORHEESVILLE, NY

Private, member owned, 18 holes

	Par	Slope	Rating	Front nine	Back nine	Total
Front tees	73	125	72.1	2753	2922	5675
Middle tees	72	125	70.7	3140	3307	6447
Back tees	72	131	73.4	3469	3582	7051

CHRONOLOGY

1890 The club forms as The Albany Hunt and Country Club. The prime activity is hunting, with an occasional fox hunt and teas. There is no golf. The clubhouse is a leased tavern on the Old Schenectady Post Road.

1894 The club incorporates.

1895 The club changes its name to The Albany Country Club. The 86-acre Knowles Farm, formerly known as Wellhurst, the old homestead of William Cooper is purchased for $12,000. This property is just south of the present leased site in what was called the "sand plains" and provides a pond for skating and hockey. An area known as Cathedral Woods is also in this plot. Tennis courts are built.

1896 A nine-hole course opens. The designer is Devereux Emmet and the length is approximately 2600 yards. The main farmhouse is converted into a clubhouse and a major dining room addition is built by John Waldbillig, father of Jerry. Caddies are dressed in full uniforms of blue French blouses and red capes.

1900 Harry Vardon sets the course record with a 70, two rounds of 35.

1904 The Hendrickson property and part of the Seely farm are purchased to provide land for a second nine.

1954   A five-year plan to renovate and modernize the clubhouse is completed. The plan is developed by Club President Dwight LaDu. Under the direction of pro and greenskeeper Willie Ogg, the course is partially redesigned.

1961   New York State takes the property to build the University at Albany. The State offers $2,119,000, but after appeals the club is awarded $3,602,806 in 1963. The land is leveled and the clubhouse burned down.

1962   The club purchases the present 500-acre site in Voorheesville. While the new course is being constructed, Colonie Country Club extends playing privileges to the Albany members.

1963   The front nine and clubhouse open. The course is designed by Robert Trent Jones. The clubhouse design is by W. Parker Dodge Associates and built by John P. Sewell, Inc.

1964   The second nine opens.

1988   The 9th green is completely redesigned by Brain Silva of Cornish and Silva.

1995   Major renovation of the clubhouse is designed by Walter M. Ballard Inc. of New York City and built by Sano-Rubin Construction Co.

NOTABLE PROS

Tom Creavy: c.1931.   Won the PGA Championship in 1931.

Willie Ogg: 1943-58.   Born in Scotland, he moved to the United States in 1914. In addition to being Albany's pro, he served as greenskeeper. He wrote the instruction book "Golf As I Know It" and developed the "Oggmented" irons. He died on Christmas Day in 1959 at the age of 71.

Bob Mix: 1959-80.   Served four years at the old club and then assisted in the smooth transition to the new location where he served for 18 more years. There is a junior tournament in his honor.

David Neavatt: 1987-97.   USGA Junior Amateur Champion 1974.

OUTSTANDING MEMBERS

Billy Shields: New York State Amateur Champion in 1951, 1952 and 1955. In 1952, he was the low qualifier for the US Open and a quarter finalist in both the British and French Amateur Championships. He also played in the Masters that year.

NOTES

Albany has hosted the New York State Amateur Championship twice, in 1977 and 1990.

Prior to purchasing the Knowles Farm in 1895, some members wanted to move to the Pierson Farm on New Scotland Road because the road was better and their carriages would not get scratched by the brambles.

In the early years, Western Avenue was a toll road. The club arranged to have members' tolls paid in one lump sum. Eventually the club's stage was allowed to pass toll free.

Albany golfers in the 1890's were called "British Cranks."

AMSTERDAM MUNICIPAL GOLF COURSE

AMSTERDAM, NY

Public, 18 holes

	Par	Slope	Rating	Front nine	Back nine	Total
Front tees	74	110	70.2	2778	2574	5352
Back tees	71	120	70.2	3317	3053	6370

CHRONOLOGY

1938   The course designed by Robert Trent Jones opens.

1992   An automatic irrigation system is installed.

NOTES

Arthur Carter, the mayor of Amsterdam from 1936 to 1943, worked with the WPA to found the course.

The first group to play the course included Gene Sarazen and Bryon Nelson.

The club has a full restaurant and banquet facilities.

ANTLERS COUNTRY CLUB

FORT JOHNSON, NY

Private, member owned, 18 holes

	Par	Slope	Rating	Front nine	Back nine	Total
Front tees	72	119	69.5	2712	2575	5287
Middle tees	70	108	68.3	3166	2867	6033
Back tees	70	115	69.3	3296	3018	6314

CHRONOLOGY

1900   Designed by William H. Tucker, the course starts with five holes, expands to seven and then nine holes.

1962   Highway construction takes land from 1st and 18th holes.

1965   The clubhouse burns down. Highway money is used to build a new one.

NOTABLE PROS

John H. Lord: Long time pro at Antlers. He came from the Mohawk Golf Club in Schenectady where he was a pro at age 18. He won many NENYPGA tournaments. He had three brothers, all pros.

Frank Stuhler: Won many NENYPGA tournaments and was fifth in the Western Open.

OUTSTANDING MEMBERS

Sarah Jane Stuhler: Won NYS Junior Women's Amateur in 1969 and 1970. Also NYS Women's Amateur in 1975.

Clarence Carpenter: Low amateur in Empire State Open at Wolferts Roost.

MEMBERS WHO TURNED PRO:
Peter Baxter, Frank Conti, Howie Derrick and Diane Wilde.

NOTES

In 1913, an exhibition was played by Harry Vardon, Ted Ray, John Lord and Gil Tiffany from the Mohawk Club.

In 1998, a skins game was held with Dottie Pepper, Juli Inkster, Moira Dunn and Denise Killeen.

The course was the birthplace of the radio controlled model airplane on land that was to become the 2nd hole.

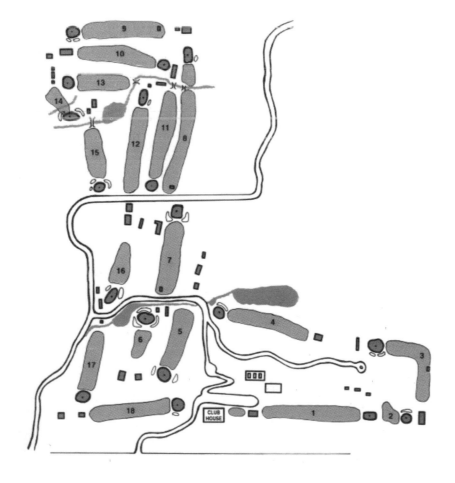

BALLSTON SPA COUNTRY CLUB

BALLSTON SPA, NY

Semi-private, 18 holes

	Par	Slope	Rating	Front nine	Back nine	Total
Front tees	74	122	70.5	2610	2870	5480
Middle tees	71	122	68.3	2790	3065	5855
Back tees	71	124	69.6	2950	3215	6165

CHRONOLOGY

1925   The club forms as the Ballston Golf Club.

1926   A nine-hole course designed by architect Jim Thompson opens.

1934   Application is made for membership in the USGA and the Women's Northeastern Golf Association.

1959   The 7th green is moved when Rt. 67 is widened.

1961   Nine holes designed by architect Gino Turchi and Armand Farina are added.

1971   The clubhouse is expanded.

1988   A water system for fairways is installed.

1995   Water for the clubhouse is piped in from the town of Milton.

NOTABLE PROS

Tim O'Connell: 1933-53.
Jim Farina: 1953-66.
Dick Osborn: 1966-85.

OUTSTANDING MEMBERS

DeForest Weed: Founder, First President.
Doug Welsh: Member for 50 years.
Neil Hodsol: Member for 50 years.
Lonnie Parks: Seven-time club champion.

NOTES

Electric carts were first allowed in 1963.

The course was the site of the NYS Golf Association Senior Women's
Championship in 1997.

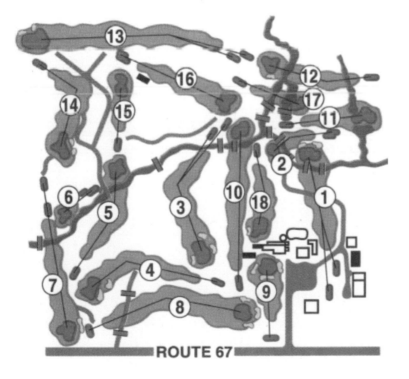

BATTENKILL COUNTRY CLUB

GREENWICH, NY

Public, 9 holes

	Par	Slope	Rating	Front nine	Back nine	Total
Front tees	71	111	68.8	2618	2520	5138
Back tees	70	117	67.6	2953	2967	5920

CHRONOLOGY

1925   The club is formed and the course opens after land along the Battenkill River is leased from the Stevens and Thompson Paper Co. The course is designed by the founders: Allan Hand, Edward Jones, Leroy Thompson, Dr. M. Rogers and George Daisy. The course is essentially unchanged to this day.

1976   Members purchase the land from Thompson Paper.

1996   An irrigation system is installed. The club is incorporated as a non-profit corporation.

NOTABLE PROS

H. J. Duval: 1928.
Jules Marozin: 1964-71.
Russ Ebbetts: 1971-92.
Mark Jorgensen: 1995-97.
Jay Potter: 1998-present.

OUTSTANDING MEMBERS

Harry Stants: Board of Directors and President.
Ed Brophy: Associated with the club for more than 60 years as caddie, member and manager.

NOTES

The land was originally an Indian campground and later a farm.

In 1954, Sig Makovsky set the course record of 61 during an ENYGA Tournament.

Obie Brundage was the greenskeeper from 1928 to 1972.

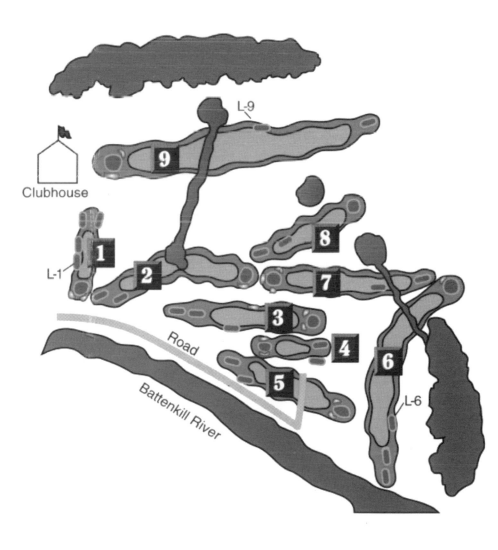

BAY MEADOWS GOLF CLUB

QUEENSBURY, NY

Public, 9 holes

	Par	Slope	Rating	Front nine	Back nine	Total
Front tees	78	na	na	2595	2595	5190
Back tees	70	117	68.7	3155	3155	6310

CHRONOLOGY

1953   The course is designed and built by Warren Gallagher, the owner.

1960's   A par 29 course is added.

1986   The club is purchased by Garth and James Allen from Gallagher's widow. Walter Romaine is hired to manage the operation.

1987   A new clubhouse and restaurant are built. The restaurant closes after a few years.

1990   The par 29 course closes to free the land for development.

NOTES

Warren Gallagher was a pro/teacher at Pinebrook and Kingsboro before starting Bay Meadows.

Walter Romaine manages the course and clubhouse as well as being grounds superintendent and greenskeeper.

BEND OF THE RIVER GOLF CLUB

HADLEY, NY

Public, 9 holes

	Par	Slope	Rating	Front nine	Back nine	Total
Front tees	74	108	66.6	2315	2540	4855
Back tees	70	110	67.0	2720	2885	5605

CHRONOLOGY

1925   The club forms as the Luzerne Villa Country Club. Steve Carhhart is the founder and course designer.

1926   The course opens.

1970   The club incorporates. Members purchase the property from Joe and Marion Hanlon, who had owned it for more than 30 years. The name changes to Bend of the River.

1990-4   A water system for the entire course is installed.

1998   New tees are built for holes 7 and 9.

NOTES

The course name comes from the fact that the clubhouse is on a bend of the Hudson River.

The signature hole is a scenic par 3 water hole.

Night tournaments are conducted once a month during the summer with glow balls.

Bend of the River caters to the new golfer and runs special programs for children.

Bend of the River hosts an American Legion Tournament each year as well as a Ladies Invitational.

BLACKHEAD MOUNTAIN COUNTRY CLUB

ROUND TOP, NY

Public, 9 holes

	Par	Slope	Rating	Front nine	Back nine	Total
Front tees	72	123	69.8	2642	2642	5284
Middle tees	72	123	67.2	2976	2976	5952
Back tees	72	126	68.0	3121	3121	6242

CHRONOLOGY

1990   The club forms and the course opens. Ewald, Waltraud, Edward and Peter Maassmann are the founders. Nicholas Psiahas is the architect. Edward Maassmann is the course superintendent.

NOTABLE PROS

Peter Maassmann has been the pro since 1990.

BRIAR CREEK GOLF CLUB

PRINCETOWN, NY

Public, 18 holes

	Par	Slope	Rating	Front nine	Back nine	Total
Front tees	71	na	na	2605	2582	5187
Back tees	70	na	na	2842	2825	5667

CHRONOLOGY

1961   Ponderosa Country Club forms and a nine-hole course opens.

1964   The club is sold and the name changed to Knights of St. Johns.

1982   The club is sold and the name changed to Sycamore Greens.

1986   Nine holes designed by Phil Greenwood and Robert W. Parks are added.

1994   The club is sold and the name changed to Briar Creek Golf Club.

NOTES

In 1994, the club was purchased by the Sise family.

The name Briar Creek comes from the stream running through the course.

BROOKHAVEN GOLF CLUB

GREENFIELD CENTER, NY
Semi-private, 18 holes

	Par	Slope	Rating	Front nine	Back nine	Total
Front tees	70	112	68.3	2661	2145	4806
Middle tees	71	121	69.5	3262	2879	6141
Back tees	71	125	71.3	3456	3071	6527

CHRONOLOGY

1960   The club is formed by O.B.Beyer Recreation Park, Inc. The founders are Herbert Edwards, Robert St. Lawrence, John Wheeler and William Burmester.

1963   The clubhouse and the nine-hole course designed by George Pulver opens.

1967   Four new holes are constructed to create a 13-hole course. Members play the first five original holes, and then either the four new holes or the four original holes. Tournaments use the nine original holes.

1971   The course expands to 18 holes. The front nine is the first five original holes and the four holes built in 1967. The back nine is the four original holes and five new holes. All holes are designed by Pulver. A 40' by 70' banquet hall is added to the clubhouse.

NOTABLE PROS

George Pulver: 1961-85.   Designed the golf course and supervised the greenskeepers. Charter member of the PGA.

NOTES

The course has 10 doglegs, six water holes and plenty of hazards. The course rating (71.3) was the second highest in the Capital Region in 1992. The course record is 69 by a pro.

Water is obtained from a creek that runs through the property and also serves as a hazard on some of the holes.

Dorothy Pepper, the grandmother of pro Dottie Pepper, was a charter member of Brookhaven and started Dottie playing golf.

In 1990, a mini-tour event was held for players who aspire to play on the PGA Senior Tour. It was set up as a Pro-Am. Pros said that Brookhaven was a course where you used all the clubs in your bag.

BRUNSWICK GREENS GOLF COURSE

TROY, NY

Public, 9 hole executive course

	Par	Front nine	Back nine	Total
Tees	56	1467	1349	2816

CHRONOLOGY

1993   The club forms and the clubhouse is built.

1994   The course opens. The founders are Al, Dolores, Denise and Rick Riccardi. The course design is by Al Riccardi, Don Lampert and Richard Danskin.

NOTABLE PROS

Frank Lamiano: PGA pro.

NOTES

The complex has a 300-yard driving range with 22 bi-level stalls, an 18-hole miniature golf course, pro shop and clubhouse with banquet facilities.

This new club has already added an unusual human interest story to its history. A member proposed to his girl friend by placing a diamond ring in the 2nd hole. When she made the putt, she found the ring.

Burden Lake Country Club

NASSAU, NY

Semi-private, 9 holes

	Par	Slope	Rating	Front nine	Back nine	Total
Front tees	72	na	na	2468	2427	4895
Back tees	72	128	68	3048	3056	6104

CHRONOLOGY

1925   The club forms and the course opens as part of the Totem Lodge.

1950   The clubhouse is expanded.

1978   The clubhouse is expanded again.

1983   Ron Choquette purchases the club.

NOTABLE PROS

Ron Choquette: 1983-present. Owner and Class "A" PGA Professional.

NOTES

Burden Lake, now with 170 acres, plans to have 18 holes by 2000 and to triple the size of the clubhouse.

The club has about 200 members. Approximately 20,000 rounds are played per year on the nine-hole course.

Burden Lake has a full service restaurant, bar and banquet facilities that are open to the public. The club can host wedding receptions, reunions and golf outings.

CANAJOHARIE COUNTRY CLUB

CANAJOHARIE, NY

Semi-private, 18 holes

	Par	Slope	Rating	Front nine	Back nine	Total
Front tees	72	115	68.5	2480	2664	5144
Middle tees	71	115	67.9	3005	2849	5854
Back tees	71	118	69.0	3250	2896	6146

CHRONOLOGY

1939   The club forms and a nine-hole course designed by Scott North, the first pro, opens.

1991   The second nine, designed by John North, the son of Scott, opens. This becomes the front nine and the original nine becomes the back nine. A water system for tees and greens is installed for this nine.

NOTES

Craig Wood and Paul Runyon played an exhibition on the course in 1941.

Doug Mochrie was the pro from 1979-80.

Mark Lane became the pro in 1991 when the new nine was built.

The club has a full restaurant, bar and banquet facilities that are open to the public.

CATSKILL GOLF CLUB

CATSKILL, NY

Semi-private, member owned, 9 holes

	Par	Slope	Rating	Front nine	Back nine	Total
Front tees	72	119	70.6	2763	2701	5464
Back tees	71	117	68.7	3138	3018	6156

CHRONOLOGY

1927   The club forms and a course designed by James Thompson opens.

1928   The club incorporates as the Catskill Golf Club, Inc.

1997   Construction of a new nine designed by Geoffrey Cornish begins. Completion is expected in 2000.

NOTABLE PROS

Bill Gressick: Past member of the national board of directors of the PGA.

OUTSTANDING MEMBERS

Dr. Mahlon Atkinson: One of the founders of the club who took an active interest in the operation. His support helped the club to survive the Depression and World War II. The club's main event each year is a memorial tournament in his honor.

NOTES

The club hosts the Catskill Pro-Am each August. Past players included Ken Green, Jeff Sluman, Mark Calcavecchia, Scott Gump and Darrell Kestner.

CHRISTMAN'S WINDHAM HOUSE

WINDHAM, NY
Public, 18 holes

	Par	Slope	Rating	Front nine	Back nine	Total
Front tees	70	na	na	1800	2479	4279
Middle tees	70	101	66.0	2310	2940	5250
Back tees	70	105	69.0	2310	3370	5680

CHRONOLOGY

1965 After selling his dairy herd, Bill Christman builds three holes on existing corn fields; holes are open to resort guests.

1965-75 Stanley Christman adds six holes to the private course for resort guests.

1988 A public nine-hole course redesigned by Stanley Christman opens. A water system for tees and greens is added. Carts are used for the first time.

1991 The Roland Stafford Golf School begins operation. A driving range, sand bunkers and a 10,000 square-foot putting green are added.

1996 A second nine holes designed and built by Brian Christman open. The son of Stanley, he holds a degree in landscape architecture from Cornell University. All nine holes have an irrigation system.

NOTES

The Windham House, opened in 1805, is the oldest continuously operated resort in the Catskills.

The Christman family purchased the property in 1952. The resort has 49 rooms and a full service restaurant.

The front nine is called the Valley Course and the back nine the Mountain Course.

The club has a covered driving range, practice trap and four putting greens.

CLIFTON KNOLLS GOLF CLUB

CLIFTON PARK, NY

Public, 9 hole executive course

	Par	Yards
Tees	28	1331

CHRONOLOGY

1964 A 12-hole course opens. Designed by Rob Mitchell and built by Robert Van Patten, it is connected with the Clifton Knolls development whose residents could be members.

NOTES

Land was later donated to the town and the course reduced to nine holes. An automatic water system was installed.

COBLESKILL GOLF AND COUNTRY CLUB

COBLESKILL, NY

Semi-private, member owned, 18 holes

	Par	Slope	Rating	Front nine	Back nine	Total
Front tees	72	118	68.1	2674	2257	4931
Middle tees	72	113	67.7	3071	2823	5894
Back tees	70	116	69.2	3183	2995	6178

CHRONOLOGY

1928   The club forms with 150 stockholders investing $150 each to produce starting capital of $22,500.

1929   The nine-hole course opens on Labor Day Weekend.

1992   On July 2, another nine holes are added. The holes are designed by Rick Colyer, an English teacher and secretary of the club.

NOTABLE PROS

Glen Snowden: 1993-present.

COLONIAL ACRES GOLF COURSE

GLENMONT, NY

Public, 9 hole executive course

	Par	Front nine	Back nine	Total
Front tees	58	1262	1262	2524
Back tees	54	1262	1262	2524

CHRONOLOGY

1964   The private course for 140 members is designed and built by developer James Michaels as part of a residential community of 115 homes. An automatic irrigation system is installed.

1972   Colonial Acres Association (homeowners) purchase the property from Michaels.

1977   Colonial Golf, Inc., made up of homeowners and others, purchases the property.

1987   The course opens to the public; more than 15,000 rounds are played annually.

1997   Several new tees are added and water holes expanded.

NOTES

The course has 10 acres of fairways and 17 acres of rough. The greens average 3600 square feet. There are 11 green sand traps, one fairway bunker and two water holes. Water for the irrigation system is supplied by two ponds.

In 1997, the course joined the New York State Audubon Society's Cooperative Sanctuary Project for golf courses. In 1998, it became the first executive course in the country to receive certification.

COLONIAL COUNTRY CLUB

TANNERSVILLE, NY

Public, 9 holes

	Par	Slope	Rating	Front nine	Back nine	Total
Front tees	70	103	64.8	2199	2199	4398
Back tees	70	107	65.8	2681	2681	5362

CHRONOLOGY

1929   The club incorporates as Tannersville Country Club in October. The 110 acres of land were purchased from Louis Allen and the clubhouse from Julius C. Dolan. The directors are Leroy W. Atwater, Julius C. Dolan, Aaron J. Levy, Louis Allen, Michael Lackey Jr., M. Harperin and Milo Claude Moseman. The club officers are Milo Claude Moseman, president; Michael Lackey Jr., vice president; Louis Allen, vice president; Julius C. Dolan, secretary and treasurer.

1930   The course opens on May 1. The course is open to the public, but has private memberships.

1960   The Leach family purchases the property from the estate of Milo Claude Moseman.

NOTES

When the course opened, there was a bridle path on the grounds and a miniature golf course near the main highway.

COLONIE COUNTRY CLUB

VOORHEESVILLE, NY

Private, member owned, 18 holes

	Par	Slope	Rating	Front nine	Back nine	Total
Front tees	73	125	74.9	3039	2947	5986
Middle tees	72	121	71.4	3289	3188	6477
Back tees	72	125	73.6	3561	3420	6981

CHRONOLOGY

1873   On January 26, German Jews establish the Adelphi Literary Association.
This social club eventually locates at 134 State St., the future site of the
Raleigh Hotel.

1913   The Adelphi Club purchases 57 acres at the corner of Wolf Road and
Central Avenue. A nine-hole golf course and modest clubhouse are
constructed. Jim Thompson, the pro at the Mohawk Club, is the course
designer. Adelphi Club dues include membership to the golf course.

1915   Fire destroys the clubhouse. Insurance does not cover the cost of a new
clubhouse, so the Adelphi club splits and Colonie Country Club is
created. Colonie needs more members, so men from Troy and
Schenectady are invited to join. A new clubhouse is constructed.

1921   The clubhouse is expanded to include a new dining room and large living
room.

1928   The clubhouse is remodeled and expanded again. Locker rooms for men
and women are added as well as a ladies' card room. A $500 assessment
is imposed, to be paid in five annual $100 payments.

1929   The stock market crash and the Depression make collections of the
assessment impossible, and the club closes. Some members rent rooms in
the Ten Eyck Hotel, in the name of the club, to play cards and hold
meetings.

1932   The golf course reopens.

1961   The Wolf Road site is sold to Sears for $1,337,000, more than $400,000 above the original offering price the club had established.

1963   A new course and clubhouse are constructed on a 250 acre parcel of land purchased for $120,000. Geoffry Cornish designs the course that cost approximately $350,000. Henry Blatner, a former club president, designs the new clubhouse that cost approximately $800,000, including furnishings. During the building phase, rooms are again rented in the Ten Eyck Hotel for card playing. Other courses in the area extend playing privileges while the new course is being built.

1992   Cornish is hired to review the course and finds that his original design of the greens and traps has been altered. The size of the greens has been reduced and some of the traps do not come into play. These changes in his original design are corrected, permitting more valid pin positions and better traps.

1996   Cornish is retained again to review the course. He recommends removal of some trees on holes 15 and 18, trimming of many other trees and the creation of some new tees for women. These recommendations are implemented.

1998   A major $2.3 million renovation is done on the clubhouse. Ballard and Company is the architect. In addition to refurbishing the majority of the clubhouse, a new Nineteenth Hole Grille Room is added. The Ladies' Card Room is enlarged and is now the Governors' Room for formal dining as well as cards. The renovations in the Main Dining Room include raising the dance floor so it is a one level room. The Men's and Women's Locker Rooms are completely renovated and larger wooden lockers provided. A special room for children is added and furnished suitably. In addition, an elevator is installed and a lift added at the outer entrance so the entire clubhouse is handicapped accessible.

NOTABLE PROS

Steve Hesch:	The first pro and greenskeeper lived on the property.
Bill Rapp: 1918-33.	A local pro and club maker.
Harry Yorke: 1934-51.	A former Canadian hockey player and boxer who died while the club pro.
Joe Creavy: 1952-59.	The brother of PGA Champ Tom Creavy.

Ed Bosse: 1961-91.   A graduate of Cortland State College who retired after
serving the club 30 years.

Frank Mellet: 1992-present.   A graduate of Marshall University who apprenticed
at Oak Hill in Rochester.

OUTSTANDING MEMBERS

Leonard Waldman and Alfred Sporborg were instrumental in the purchase of the
original 57 acres on Wolf Road.

Milton Alexander, Simon Rosenstock, George Simon and William Schwartz: These
men played a significant role in the sale of the old club and the building of the
new one in the early 1960's.

NOTES

In the late 1920s, Joseph Field invited some of his Schenectady friends to become
members of Colonie. They were refused. As a result they started Shaker Ridge
Country Club.

In 1961, New York State took over the old Albany Country Club. Colonie extended
playing privileges to Albany members while their new course was being built in
Voorheesville. When the old Colonie course was purchased by Sears, Albany
extended playing privileges to Colonie members while their new course was being
built in Voorheesville.

Gov. Herbert Lehman was an honorary member and often played golf at Colonie in
the 1920s.

In 1963, Gene Sarazen opened play at the new course. He is quoted as saying
"You have Tiffany greens and Woolworth traps."

In 1978, Gloria Hatch was the first woman elected to the Board of Governors. In
1998, the 18-member Board is composed of five women and 13 men.

In 1992, Colonie Country Club may have been the first area private country club
to establish open tee times for men and women on weekends as well as week days.

COLUMBIA GOLF AND COUNTRY CLUB

CLAVERACK, NY

Private, member owned, 18 holes

	Par	Slope	Rating	Front nine	Back nine	Total
Front tees	71	120	70.0	2549	2764	5313
Back tees	70	113	68.5	2978	3056	6034

CHRONOLOGY

c.1899   The Glenwood Golf Links are built on Worth Avenue, the future site of the New York State Training School for Girls. The property was owned by the McIntyre family. The original course has six holes and is later expanded to eight, using land that is now part of the Ten Broeck Orchard.

1902   In June, The Columbia Country Club is organized and leased as The Glenwood Links.

c.1910   The membership outgrows Glenwood and leases land on Rt. 66, formerly Union Turnpike. Nine holes and a modest clubhouse are built. (The clubhouse exists today as a private residence.)

c.1917   World War I forces the club to close.

1919   The Henry Avery Homestead of 150 acres, the club's present site, is purchased. The stock corporation is formed.

1920   Nine holes are constructed and the old farmhouse is refurbished into a clubhouse. Hal Purdy is the designer. This is the beginning of the current club.

1939   Columbia is changed from a stock corporation to a membership corporation.

1963   A new nine is added. The first foursome is Gene Sarazen, Club Pro Eddie Brown, Bill Gressick of Catskill and Claude Young of Winding Brook. A water system is installed.

NOTABLE PROS

Eddie Brown: 1930-70. He not only served as pro and supervised the greens crew, but was a plumber, electrician, carpenter, painter and mason.

OUTSTANDING MEMBERS

Gene Sarazen

NOTES

When the club was started, it was the time of the "Gibson Girl," and women players wore a scarlet coat with brass buttons and a white pique skirt. Men wore a Norfolk jacket and knickers.

Caddies were used in the early days and clubs consisted of a driver, cleek, niblik, brassie, wedge and putter.

In 1919, when the present site was purchased, the initiation was $10. Annual dues for men were $25, women $15, couple $35, and children $10. A family membership cost $50.

The Board favored getting a liquor license in the 1930s, but the members did not approve until 1953.

A swimming pool was proposed in 1935, but was not built until 1953.

The annual better ball tournament was instituted in 1959 and continues to this day.

COUNTRY CLUB OF TROY

TROY, NY

Private, member owned, 18 holes

	Par	Slope	Rating	Front nine	Back nine	Total
Front tees	74	122	73.0	2681	2868	5549
Middle tees	71	119	69.8	3061	3023	6084
Back tees	71	122	71.3	3269	3143	6412

CHRONOLOGY

1925   The club is formed, founded by Charles E. Stone, Frank Norton and Livingston W. Houston.

1927   A course designed by Walter Travis and a clubhouse designed by Pliny Rogers both open.

1951   "Chocolate drops," stone mounds that were covered with dirt when the course was built, are removed and replaced with traps.

1961   The cocktail lounge is built, replacing the flagstone terrace.

1968   An automated irrigation system is installed.

1984   Geoffrey S. Cornish creates a golf course master plan.

NOTABLE PROS

Edward Schultz: 1927-57.   He was the first pro and served for 30 years. He came from the Van Schaick Island Course in Cohoes.

OUTSTANDING MEMBERS

Pierce H. (Bud) Russell: 1934-69.   Won the Club Championship 16 times, the Governor's Cup 14 times and the Invitational five times.

NOTES

The original land, 170 acres, was purchased from the Forest Park Cemetery. Later, additional land was purchased to bring the total to 250 acres.

Walter Travis, the course designer, did not get to see the course completed. He died in August of 1927.

The stock market crash of 1929 and the Depression reduced the membership. Fees had to be lowered to attract new members, but the club remained open. During Prohibition, members brought their own stimulants to the club.

Walter Hagen, Horton Smith and Bobby Locke all played the course.

In the early 1930s, caddies were paid $1.10 for 18 holes. The extra 10¢ went into a caddy fund to reward the best caddies.

In 1984, the club hosted the New York State Amateur tournament.

The course has small undulating greens and multiple tee locations.

The clubhouse consists of several buildings rather than one large mansion, which was the custom when the clubhouse was built. The living room has hand hewn beams that resemble the inverted hull of a sailing vessel. The clubhouse overlooks the Poestenkill Gorge and Grafton Mountain.

The Country Club of Troy

TROY, NEW YORK
FOUNDED 1927

ORIGINAL GOLF COURSE DESIGN BY WALTER TRAVIS

CRANWELL RESORT AND GOLF CLUB

LENOX, MA

Resort, 18 holes

	Par	Slope	Rating	Front nine	Back nine	Total
Front tees	72	129	72.4	2877	2725	5602
Middle tees	70	125	70.0	3236	2933	6169
Back tees	70	125	70.0	3311	3035	6346

CHRONOLOGY

1928   The club is formed as the Berkshire Hunt and Country Club. The owner is Woodson R. Ogleby, a former New York Congressman, who purchased the property (called Wyndhurst) at a foreclosure sale. (He planned a private club for 1600 families that never materialized.) The 18-hole course designed by architects Wayne E. Stiles and John R. Van Cleek opens.

1933   Litigation and debt force the club to be sold to Edward Cranwell for about $9,000 in back taxes. Cranwell was probably a financial backer of Ogleby.

1939   Cranwell donates the property to the Jesuits for a preparatory school. The main building is renamed St. Joseph's Hall. The golf course remains open.

1970s   The school is closed and Cranwell reopens as a resort.

1992   The building housing the pro shop and pub is damaged by fire.

1993   Burack Investments becomes the new owner and starts a major upgrade program.

1994   The old gym is converted into an indoor golf center.

1996   An irrigation system is installed for 12 of the 18 holes.

NOTES

The first recorded ownership of the "Hill" was in 1770. The owners were Timothy Wray and Samuel Jerome, the latter the great, great grandfather of Mrs. Randolph Churchill, mother of Winston Churchill.

On June 13, 1803, the "Hill" was sold to Ezra Blossom for $70. He named it Blossom Hill.

Charles Hotchkiss, the second Head of the Lenox Academy, purchased the land on April 30, 1850. In September 1853, Hotchkiss sold the property to Henry Ward Beecher, brother of Harriet Beecher Stowe, for $4,500. Reverend Beecher built the first house on the land and renamed the "Hill" Blossom Farm.

Reverend Beecher sold the property to Gen. John F. Rathbone for $8,000. The General renamed the property Wyndhurst, and by 1882 it was an established resort.

In 1893, Rathbone sold Wyndhurst to Mrs. Sloane for $50,000. The Sloanes tore down the cottages and built a magnificent Tudor mansion. On July 4, 1897, they entertained President and Mrs. McKinley.

The holes on the course are separated by woodlands and, with the hilly terrain, spectacular views are available.

1 Par 4

2 Par 4

3 Par 3

4 Par 5

5 Par 3

6 Par 4

7 Par 4

8 Par 4

9 Par 4

CRONIN'S GOLF RESORT

WARRENSBURG, NY

Resort, 18 holes

	Par	Slope	Rating	Front nine	Back nine	Total
Front tees	71	na	68.6	3123	2634	5757
Back tees	70	119	68.3	3283	2838	6121

CHRONOLOGY

1930 A nine-hole course named the Queen Village opens. It is owned, built and designed by Mark Cassidy. Patrick Cronin, grandfather of the present owners, aids in the design. He was the superintendent of the Glens Falls Country Club.

1945 Robert Cronin, son of Patrick and a golf pro, purchases the course from Mark Cassidy.

1966 Nine holes are added. Robert Cronin is the designer.

1970s Ice from the Hudson River damages the course.

1980 Because of the constant ice damage, part of the course is redesigned on higher ground.

1988 James and John Cronin, sons of Robert, purchase the course. Robert retires as a golf pro.

1989 The 3rd green is redesigned.

1994 A pond is added to the 8th hole.

1998 The 7th green is redesigned.

NOTABLE PROS

Robert Cronin: 1945-88.   Golf pro and owner.

NOTES

Cronin's has 15 housekeeping cottages and eight motel units that can house up to 100 people on the property. They have banquet facilities for golf outings and other groups.

The resort was called Vacationland from 1968 to 1988 when the name was changed to Cronin's Golf Resort.

Season golf passes are available.

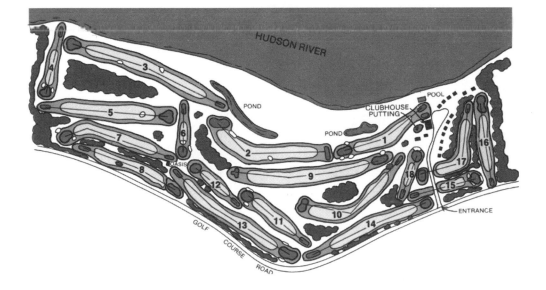

Duffer's Den

Saratoga Springs, NY

Public, 9 hole executive course

	Par	Front nine	Back nine	Total
Tees	54	868	868	1736

CHRONOLOGY

1975   The club forms as Duffer's Den and the course opens. The founder is Donald Pepper, the father of LPGA Pro Dottie Pepper. A water system is installed.

1979   The property is purchased by Milton Burke Sr.

1980   A 400-foot grass driving range is constructed.

1984-86 With the input of George Pulver, all the greens are enlarged and the 7th and 8th greens relocated.

1987   Mike Dennis of McGregor Links purchases the property, but Milton Burke continues to operate it.

NOTABLE PROS

George Pulver: 1980-85.   Helped to redesign the course and was a teacher of Dottie Pepper.

Bill Potter: 1988-91.   Author of "Swing Your Own Swing."

Milton Burke Sr: 1991-present. Instrumental in organizing youth golf programs through local schools and junior golf leagues. A graduate of the Golf Works Professional Club, he conducts adult education programs in golf instruction.

NOTES

The course was built with lights for night play. Milton Burke had them removed because people would play until 1 a.m. He donated the lights to charity.

When Burke purchased the property, he intended to run antique shows, which he did. However, so many people wanted to play golf that he kept the golf course operating.

PGA Pro Ray Floyd makes an annual visit to practice on the range.

Many celebrities, horse trainers and owners play the course during the Saratoga racing season.

Dutchaven Golf Course

SCHAGHTICOKE, NY

Public, 9 hole executive course

	Par	Front nine	Back nine	Total
Tees	58	1480	1486	2966

CHRONOLOGY

1963   The club forms and the course opens. The founder and course designer is Nicholas Schnurr.

1988   The club is purchased by James Carey. Several improvements are made, including a new 3rd fairway, and pond with a fountain.

1993   A water system is installed for the entire course. The original system only covered the greens.

NOTES

The course is located only four miles from the Grandma Moses Homestead.

The course is ideal for the beginner or someone who wants to work on the short game. Very reasonable greens fees for either nine or 18 holes.

EAGLE CREST GOLF CLUB

BALLSTON LAKE, NY

Public, 18 holes

	Par	Slope	Rating	Front nine	Back nine	Total
Front tees	72	117	68.6	2626	2456	5082
Middle tees	72	121	69.8	3162	3081	6243
Back tees	72	126	72.4	3404	3410	6814

CHRONOLOGY

1963   The club is formed as the Northway Heights Golf Club by the Gino Turchi family.

1965   The course designed by Gino Turchi opens on June 12 with nine holes.

1967   The second nine, also designed by Turchi, opens on July 13.

1991   The property is sold in February to the William Paulsen family and the name is changed to Eagle Crest.

NOTABLE PROS

Jim Jeffers: 1993-present.

NOTES

The course hosted the New York State Amateur in 1994 and the Mid-Amateur Qualifier in 1996.

The course hosted a North Atlantic Pro Tour stop in 1997 and 1998.

Edison Club

REXFORD, NY

Private, member owned, 27 holes

	Par	Slope	Rating	First nine	Third nine	Total
Front tees	72	123	71.7	2837	2727	5564
Middle tees	72	118	70.5	3148	3255	6403
Back tees	72	121	71.9	3278	3426	6704

CHRONOLOGY

1904   The club leases the former site of the Mohawk Golf Club at the corner of Rosa Road and Nott Street when Mohawk moves to its present site.

1908   The club is incorporated by General Electric as a social organization for its employees. The first constitution reads "The particular objects for which the corporation is to be formed are to encourage the playing of athletic games and sports; to encourage canoeing, rowing, sculling, water boating, sailing and aquatic games and sports." The clubhouse is located on the site of the present WRGB television studio. There is also a boathouse on the Mohawk River.

1927   The club moves to its present site in Rexford. The farmhouse is converted to a clubhouse and the golf course opens. The architect for the course is Devereux Emmet.

1948   A new clubhouse is constructed.

1968   Members purchase the club from General Electric.

NOTABLE PROS

Alex B McIntyre: 1927-50.
Robert Haggerty, Sr.: 1950-72.

OUTSTANDING MEMBERS

Karsten Solheim: Worked for General Electric and then founded the Ping
                     Company.
Lou Torre: Schenectady golf writer.

NOTES

Edison has three nines. The figures above are for the first and third nines which
have the highest slope figure of any combination from the back tees. The other
combinations are as follows:

	1st/2nd nines	2nd/3rd nines
Front tees	72.0/123	71.2/118
Middle tees	69.2/116	69.7/114
Back tees	70.5/119	71.2/117

EVERGREEN COUNTRY CLUB

CASTLETON, NY
Semi-private, 36 holes

	Par	Slope	Rating	Front nine	Back nine	Total
Front tees	75	133	76.5	2889	2705	5594
Middle tees	72	127	72.0	3355	3377	6732
Back tees	72	131	73.5	3647	3597	7244

CHRONOLOGY

1961   Construction begins.

1963   The course opens on July 19 with 18 holes; nine more are added later. The club has an Olympic size swimming pool.

1977   The clubhouse is destroyed by fire in May.

1978   The clubhouse is rebuilt on the same site.

1981   Nine local businessmen buy the property and rename the club Schodack Country Club.

1985   Paul Roth purchases the property.

1988   Joe Bove, a PGA professional, and Fred Kassner, owner of Liberty Travel, buy the property and change the name to Evergreen Country Club.

NOTABLE PROS
Warren Davis: 1963-1982.
Joseph Bove: 1988-present.

NOTES

Tea dances were held Sunday evenings with the big band sound. The dance floor was the largest in the area. International dinners were held once a month.

Charity tournaments were held for the Association for Blind Golfers.

A snowmobile club was formed with trails and a race track on the course.

The clubhouse has a full service bar, restaurant and banquet facilities.

FREAR PARK GOLF COURSE

TROY, NY

Public, 18 holes

	Par	Slope	Rating	Front nine	Back nine	Total
Front tees	73	111	69.2	2576	2751	5327
Middle tees	71	106	66.5	2862	3041	5903
Back tees	71	109	68.0	2972	3262	6234

CHRONOLOGY

1931   A nine-hole course designed by John S. Melville opens.

1962   A second nine designed by Robert Trent Jones is added.

1982   A new water system for the entire course is installed.

NOTABLE PROS

John Moynihan: 1932-78.

OUTSTANDING MEMBERS

L. G. Christie, C. H. Wilson, A. E. Halligan and W. T. Sannons were the first members and the first golfers to play the course in 1931.

NOTES

The course has a hilly front nine and a flat, open back nine. The four par 3s are among the toughest in the area. There are three doglegs and two water holes. The 5th requires a carry over a deep ravine.

FRENCH'S HOLLOW FAIRWAYS

GUILDERLAND CENTER, NY

Public, 9 holes

	Par	Front nine	Back nine	Total
Tees	74	3145	2980	6125

CHRONOLOGY

1971   The clubhouse is built and the course opens. The founders are Dr. Z. John Betlejeski (who designed the course) and Richard Betlejeski. The course is built on the family dairy farm.

NOTES

The original unheated cinder block building is still used as the clubhouse. A space heater has been added, but when the temperature falls below freezing they must close.

In the spring, huge snapping turtles crawl from the Watervliet Reservoir across the 5th fairway to lay their eggs.

The present owner is Louise B. Betlejeski.

GALWAY GOLF COURSE

GALWAY, NY

Public, 9 hole executive course

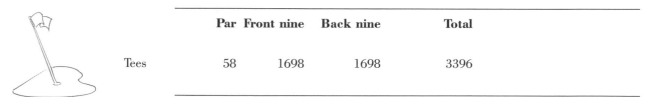

	Par	Front nine	Back nine	Total
Tees	58	1698	1698	3396

CHRONOLOGY

1967   The club forms and the course designed by George Wedekind opens.

NOTABLE PROS

Dr. Anthony Pacelli: Retired from the State University of New York, he is the club instructor.

NOTES

The founders were George Wedekind and Carl Elmendorf.

Over the years the course has gradually changed from a small par 3 to a 1700 yard executive course. The club caters to seniors and beginners. It is considered very beginner friendly.

Plans include two new holes that will change the configuration, but still remain a nine-hole course.

GLENS FALLS COUNTRY CLUB

GLENS FALLS, NY

Private, member owned, 18 holes

	Par	Slope	Rating	Front nine	Back nine	Total
Front tees	73	122	71.4	2632	2820	5452
Middle tees	71	124	69.2	3020	3105	6125
Back tees	71	127	70.9	3177	3299	6476

CHRONOLOGY

1912   The club forms.

1914   The nine-hole course designed by Donald Ross opens.

1922   Nine holes designed by Ross and Walter Hatch are added.

1923   The clubhouse burns down on April 14.

1924   A new clubhouse is built.

NOTABLE PROS

Ben Lord Sr.: 1917-56.
Al Stein: 1966-80.
Tom Haggerty: 1981-present.

NOTES

From 1929 to 1939, the Glens Falls Open was played. This was a PGA tour event
and attracted the best players, including Walter Hagen, Ben Hogan, Byron Nelson
and Sam Snead.

HIAWATHA TRAILS GOLF COURSE

GUILDERLAND, NY

Public, 18 hole executive course

	Par	Front nine	Back nine	Total
Front tees	57	1235	1016	2251
Back tees	57	1315	1016	2331

CHRONOLOGY

1960   A nine-hole course, founded and designed by Dominic Ferraioli, opens and a clubhouse is built.

1970   A second nine, also designed by Ferraioli, opens.

1995   A complete irrigation system is installed.

NOTES

The owner previously had a nine-hole course and driving range on the opposite side of the road. This was built in the 1950s. The property was sold to the Guilderland School District for the new school.

The course has a pond and a creek that crosses five holes.

HILAND GOLF CLUB

Queensbury, NY
Semi-private, 18 holes

	Par	Slope	Rating	Front nine	Back nine	Total
Front tees	72	123	72.5	2839	2838	5677
Middle tees	72	130	71.4	3175	3198	6373
Back tees	72	133	72.5	3321	3311	6632

CHRONOLOGY

1988-89 The club forms and the clubhouse and course designed by Stephen Kay
is opened by founder Gary Bowen, a private developer.

1995   The property is purchased by Family Golf Centers Inc.

NOTES

The clubhouse won the 1990 award from the National Association of Home
Builders for the best design in the United States.

Hiland hosted the 1992 New York State Open.

The Hiland practice facility was selected as one of the top 88 in America for
1996-97 by "Golf Ranges of America." It features a heated indoor and elevated
outdoor driving range.

The club has full service restaurant and banquet facilities that are open to the
public. In 1996, the Hiland Family Golf Center was opened. The Center provides
individual and group instruction as well as offering one-day and three-day golf
schools.

In 1998, Hiland hosted the International Junior Golf tournament.

HILLCREST GOLF AND COUNTRY CLUB

SCHENECTADY, NY

Public, 9 holes

	Par	Front nine	Back nine	Total
Tees	74	3132	3132	6264

CHRONOLOGY

1961   The course opens.

HOLLAND MEADOWS GOLF COURSE

GLOVERSVILLE, NY

Public, 18 hole executive course

	Par	Front nine	Back nine	Total
Front tees	63	1493	1840	3333
Back tees	59	1493	1840	3333

CHRONOLOGY

1962   The club forms as the White Holland House Executive Golf Course. The nine holes are designed by Walter Coons.

1968   Nine more par 3 holes are added.

1972   The course becomes an 18-hole executive course after being expanded and redesigned by Coons.

1981   The property is purchased by Dennis Sniezyk, an employee since 1970.

1996   A new pro shop featuring golf simulators is added.

NOTABLE PROS

Frank L. McGuinness: 1973-91.   A golf pro for 68 years who had taught with Tommy Armour in Florida for many winters. He taught golf until the day before his death.

NOTES

The club has a driving range and practice putting green.

HOOSICK FALLS COUNTRY CLUB

HOOSICK FALLS, NY

Semi-private, 9 holes

	Par	Slope	Rating	Front nine	Back nine	Total
Front tees	68	109	63.3	2014	2152	4166
Back tees	68	113	65.9	2788	2767	5555

CHRONOLOGY

1910   The course and the clubhouse open. The founders and course designers are Willis Heaton, A. H. Allen, M.C. Milliman, Danforth Geer, Louis Haussler, E. H. McLean Jr. and George Green.

1926   The Hoosick Valley Invitation Golf Tournament for Women is inaugurated.

1975   A new clubhouse opens. Membership is 142. The hope is that the new clubhouse will increase membership to 175.

NOTABLE PROS

Jack Parr: 1910-17.
Mike Bachorz: Early 1930s to 1994.
Miles Nolan: 1995-present.

NOTES

The original clubhouse cost $650 to build plus another $50 for painting and completion. The golf course cost $800 to build. Some golf holes belonging to Walter A. Wood may have already existed when the course was built.

Dues the first year were $25 for an active member. Associate dues were $15 for a family, $10 for a man and $5 for a woman.

Jack Parr (great name for a golf pro), the first pro, was paid $40 per month with a $10 bonus if the club did well.

In 1980, Francis J. "Mike" Bachorz was honored by the club for almost 50 years of service. Mr. and Mrs. Bachorz were given life memberships in the club as well as many other gifts. A plaque honoring him is displayed in the clubhouse.

The club was elected to the United States Lawn Tennis Association in 1914. At the grand opening in 1910, a tennis match was played against the North Adams Country Club.

The Hoosick Valley Invitation Golf Tournament, started in 1926, was a major event for women in the area. It was a two-day tournament held in July. There was a nine-hole qualifier, followed by three more nine-hole matches. The entry fee was $2. The first winner was Miss Margaret Hanson from the Mohawk Golf Club. In 1927, the winner was Mrs. Robert Meckley, also from the Mohawk Club. By 1928, the qualifier was 18 holes, followed by three 18-hole matches for the first division. Two women played 72 holes in two days. (The other divisions played nine-hole matches.) The entry fee was now $2.50. The event did not last. In 1930, there was a one-day "open golf day" for women with an entry fee of 50¢ and lunch for 75¢. Interesting to note the lunch cost more than the tournament.

Club founder Louis Haussler is the grandfather of Dennis McEvoy, a present member who supplied much of this history.

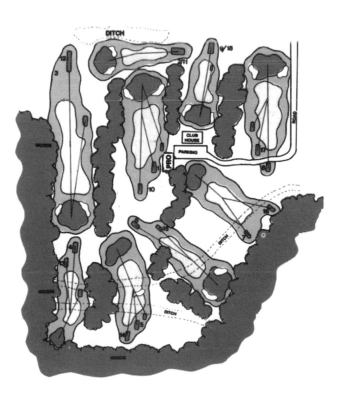

Kingsboro Golf Club

GLOVERSVILLE, NY

Public, 9 holes

	Par	Slope	Rating	Front nine	Back nine	Total
Front tees	74	na	na	2910	2885	5795
Back tees	73	na	na	3050	3070	6120

CHRONOLOGY

1931   The course opens on July 4. Carlton Sanford is the founder. He purchased 65 acres of the Burr Farm. James Floyd and Hugo Kuhne of the Sir William Johnson Country Club are the architects. Felix Mercer of Schenectady is the first pro. The club has 15 members the first year.

1932   Warren Gallagher is hired as pro on July 4. A water system is installed.

1933   Sanford sets up a Board of Governors to run the club activities. Layton E. Brown is the first chairman and serves to 1936. He is followed by Robert Heagle.

1934   A Board of Governors for women members is appointed. Mildred Holmes is the first chair and serves until 1937. Gaynell E. Evans follows her.

1935   A clubhouse is built and furnished by the members. Dining services are instituted. Seventy steel lockers are installed for the men and 30 for the women.

1937   Membership reaches 250.

1989   Paul Jaycox purchases the course and becomes the pro. He has been a pro since 1974.

NOTES

During the 1930's, five new holes were constructed. Cal Winsbro was the architect.

Clarence Brown, an undertaker, was the first person to play the course. The first member was Harold V. Wessels, an insurance agent.

Kingsboro was the originator of the Fulton County Amateur Tournament.

KINGSBORO GOLF CLUB

GLOVERSVILLE
NY 773-4600

PAUL JAYCOX
PGA PROFESSIONAL

KINGSWOOD GOLF CLUB

HUDSON FALLS, NY

Public, 18 holes

	Par	Slope	Rating	Front nine	Back nine	Total
Front tees	71	116	69.8	2665	2519	5184
Middle tees	71	123	68.8	3148	2969	6117
Back tees	71	128	71.9	3405	3166	6571

CHRONOLOGY

1991   The club forms and the course opens with Michael Woodbury as its founder and designer. An irrigation system is installed.

NOTABLE PROS

Kevin Hughes: 1991-present. Class "A" PGA Professional.

NOTES

Kingswood Golf Club features pure greens and lush Bent Grass fairways with beautiful views of the Adirondacks and Green Mountains. Water comes into play on eight holes.

The club has a driving range with grass tees as well as a sand and chipping area, a putting green and a teaching pro.

Kingswood hosted the New York State Open Qualifier in 1995 and a North Atlantic Tour event in 1997. The North Atlantic Tour Championship was held there in September 1998. Kingswood will host the 1999 New York State Women's Amateur Championship.

The Kingswood Classic started in 1992. It is a 27-hole, two-man championship. Each nine holes has a different format; scramble, better ball and alternate shot. The tournament attracts many of the best players in the area as well as golfers with high handicaps.

LEATHERSTOCKING GOLF COURSE

COOPERSTOWN, NY

Resort, 18 holes

	Par	Slope	Rating	Front nine	Back nine	Total
Front tees	72	116	69.2	2594	2660	5254
Middle tees	72	120	69.3	2996	3057	6053
Back tees	72	124	71.0	3121	3203	6324

CHRONOLOGY

1909   The club forms as the Cooperstown Country Club and the course opens. Stephen C. Clark Sr. is the founder of the course designed by Devereux Emmet.

1971   The name is changed to Leatherstocking Golf Course.

1993   An automatic water system is installed.

1998   New tees are constructed for all holes.

NOTABLE PROS

Leonard Raynor: 1918-52.

Ed Kroll: 1952-92.   Served as pro for 40 years and was instrumental in developing the Baseball Hall of Fame Golf Tournament and the Cooperstown Senior Open. His daughter, Nancy, became one of the leading women amateurs in the region.

Rick Wolcott: 1993-96.

Dan Spooner: 1997-present.

OUTSTANDING MEMBERS

Margret Neville: She won the New York State Women's Amateur Championship five times.

Jack Ryerson: He was a boy on Titanic; his father, Arthur, died in the tragedy. Arthur had been active at the Otsego Golf Course since 1904. At one time Jack was in the *Guiness Book of Records* for having played more different golf courses than anyone else in the world.

NOTES

The Otsego Golf Course, at the north end of the lake, was built in 1894. Many people from Cooperstown would travel up the lake to play. In 1898, these golfers convinced Edward S. Clark to build a nine-hole course off the road to Fly Creek. This course was called the Annex Links at Cooperstown of the Otsego Golf Club. It closed when the present Leatherstocking Course opened in 1909.

The Cooperstown Invitational was held from 1931 to 1956. In 1957, this was changed to the Otesaga Open. In 1983, the tournament was changed to the Cooperstown Senior Open and has attracted many of the best senior players in the Northeast.

The course is the site of the annual Baseball Hall of Fame Golf Tournament.

MaRia Mountain Golf Course

DUANESBURG, NY

Public, 9 holes

	Par	Yards
Front tees	36	2768
Back tees	36	3044

CHRONOLOGY

1992   The course designed by Hal Bruhnes opens.

NOTES

The course has a driving range.

McGregor Links Country Club

SARATOGA SPRINGS, NY

Private, 18 holes

	Par	Slope	Rating	Front nine	Back nine	Total
Front tees	75	125	71.6	3061	2460	5521
Middle tees	72	130	70.8	3280	3069	6349
Back tees	72	133	72.2	3390	3239	6629

CHRONOLOGY

1921   The club forms and the course opens. The founder is Sen. Edward T. Brackett. The course is designed by Devereux Emmet.

NOTABLE PROS

George Pulver: 1924-61.

NOTES

Sen. Brackett was the sponsor of legislation to create the State Reservation at Saratoga Springs in 1905 to protect the Springs.

The course was named for nearby Mount McGregor. It is located on 900 acres and has no parallel fairways.

The neo-colonial clubhouse was designed by architect Alfred Hopkins.

MEADOWGREENS GOLF CLUB

GHENT, NY

Semi-public, 9 holes

	Par	Front nine	Back nine	Total
Front tees	72	2914	2914	5828
Back tees	72	3011	3011	6022

CHRONOLOGY

1965   A nine-hole course covering 55 acres and named Cedar Meadows opens. The founders are three brothers, Basil, David and Harry Karpiak, and their brother-in-law, Phil Karmazyn. They purchased 195 acres in 1952 as a dairy farm and started building the course in 1960. An automatic irrigation system was installed at that time. The barn is used for the clubhouse and pro shop. Some 8000 rounds are played the first year.

1966   Columbia County condemns 22.6 acres for the new airport and takes an easement for another 26 acres so the planes could fly over the course. The owners sue.

1967   Twenty-five campsites are built on the property. The owners win the lawsuit, but appeal the amount of damages.

1968   A barn is converted into a restaurant. The owners are awarded $43,191 in their lawsuit. The defendants appeal, but lose.

1976   Fire burns the restaurant to the ground. The owners rebuild on the same site.

1979   The property is purchased by the Kozel family at auction.

1985   A practice putting green is added.

1986   The chipping green opens.

1991   Sand traps are added to the course.

1997   A pond is constructed on the 1st hole.

NOTES

The course is located next to the Columbia County Airport. Pilots often fly in for golf or meals.

Meadowgreens encourages youth play with special seasonal passes for student and college golfers.

MECHANICVILLE GOLF CLUB

MECHANICVILLE, NY

Semi-private, member owned, 9 holes

	Par	Slope	Rating	Front nine	Back nine	Total
Front tees	74	na	na	2930	2810	5740
Back tees	72	118	68.5	3088	3053	6141

CHRONOLOGY

1909   The club forms.

1910   The course, designed by architect Devereux Emmet and owned by the West Virginia Pulp and Paper Co., opens.

1959   The original clubhouse burns down.

1961   The present clubhouse is built.

1977   Members purchase the club from West Virginia Pulp and Paper Co.

1988   A water system is added.

1998   On May 31, a tornado strikes the course in the area of the 4th tee, uprooting numerous trees and causing extensive damage. There is no structural damage to any buildings.

NOTABLE PROS

Tommy MacKensie (Scottish born): 1930-57.
Jerry Sistito: 1963-69.
Michael Martone: 1980-91.
Tom Sullivan: 1992-present.

OUTSTANDING MEMBERS

Tim Lilac: 50-year member.
Sal Rinaldi: 50-year member.

NOTES

Members are allowed to own their own golf carts and pay a storage fee.

Walter Hagen and Horton Smith played an exhibition at the course in 1929.
Johnny Dwyer was the club pro.

The club hosted pro tournaments in the 1930's.

In 1998, Mechanicville won the Devereux Emmet Cup played at the Edison Club.
This is a tournament among clubs designed by Emmet. The team members were
Fred DeCasperis, Marty DePoalo, Bernie Murphy, Tim Nimmons, Bill Pickett, Tom
Salvadore, Jack Stone and Steve Ventresca.

MILL ROAD ACRES GOLF COURSE

LATHAM, NY

Public, 18 hole executive course

	Par	Front nine	Back nine	Total
Front tees	57	1360	1035	2395
Back tees	58	1685	1340	3025

CHRONOLOGY

1973   The club forms.

1974   Clayton and Irene Russell build the course on their family farm. He designs the course with the help of a former golf pro from the Town of Colonie Course.

1981   Robert Clickner and William Sano purchase the property and operate the course for two years.

1983   Gordon and Gloria Jevons purchase the property and are the current owners.

1995   Construction starts on a new nine.

1997   The new nine opens in August.

NOTABLE PROS

Alex Sinclair: 1984-93.   Former Schuyler Meadows golf pro.
Peter Gerard: 1994-present.   Spalding Teacher of the Year, 1996.

NOTES

The course has a driving range and a dining room with banquet facilities.

MOHAWK GOLF CLUB

SCHENECTADY, NY

Private, member owned, 18 holes

	Par	Slope	Rating	Front nine	Back nine	Total
Front tees	73	125	73.8	2984	2767	5751
Middle tees	71	123	70.6	3275	3026	6301
Back tees	71	126	72.1	3486	3185	6671

CHRONOLOGY

1898   The club forms.

1899   A nine-hole course opens on 40 acres of leased land at the corner of Rosa
Road and Nott Street. The holes range in length from 254 to 423 yards
and total 2817 yards. Original members invest $2,000 each to get
started. The clubhouse is built at a cost of $1,344.75. Membership grows
to 277.

1901   Due to the large membership, Mohawk outgrows the original site. The
155-acre Smitley Farm on Troy Road (the present location) is purchased.
The total cost for the land, course construction and new clubhouse is
$92,000. Generous members donate some of the money; the rest is
borrowed. Prior to this purchase, the club considers combining with the
Union College Pastures course to form an 18-hole course.

1904   The new 5805-yard course opens. The former site is leased to the Edison
Club.

1907   On May 21, the clubhouse burns down.

1908   On May 21, a new clubhouse opens at a cost of $57,114.48.

1909-21 Fifty-four additional acres are purchased.

1914   Four acres are sold to the City of Schenectady for the Bevis Hill
Reservoir. Mohawk is paid $5,000 and is guaranteed a water supply for
25 years.

1923   On April 26, the clubhouse is destroyed by fire.

1925   On New Year's Day, the new clubhouse opens. The cost, nearly $300,000, leaves Mohawk with substantial debt for the first time. This building is the base of the present clubhouse.

1938   Mohawk makes a film, *Lest We Forget*, which shows the early history of the club.

1957   A par 3 course opens. It is called the "wee" course.

1961   The terrace roof is added to the clubhouse.

1967   A water system is installed at a cost of approximately $100,000.

1979   Second floor bedrooms are removed from the clubhouse.

1983   The men's locker room is expanded and renovated.

1986   An ice storm damages hundreds of trees.

1990-91 Major renovation is done on the clubhouse.

NOTABLE PROS

Jim Thomson: 1918-68. Served as pro and course superintendent for 50 years.
Alex Sinclair: 1957-72.
John Maurycy: 1973-96.
Rick Wolcott: 1998-present.

OUTSTANDING MEMBERS

Billie Patten:	Club Champ 11 times between 1907-27.
Chick Eigelbach:	Club Champ 13 times between 1944-65.
Rudolph Romeling:	The 8th hole is dedicated to him.
Bill Knight:	Inventor of the Schenectady Putter and steel shafts. The 15th hole is dedicated to him.
Dick Emmet:	Greens chair from 1907-29. The 14th hole is dedicated to him.
Pat McTerney:	Greens chair from 1931-66.
Harry Summerhayes:	Charter member. The "wee" course is dedicated to him.

NOTES

The original initiation fee was $10 and annual dues were $15 for resident members. The initiation fee was waived for those who joined before May 1, 1899. Women joined as Associate members with annual dues of $7.50.

The first president was E. W. Rice, Jr., a vice president of General Electric. The turn of the century was a booming time for the City of Schenectady and the Mohawk Club did well. Total income for the first year was $4,053.05, resulting in a profit of $349.78.

When the new course was ready in 1904, some members played a cross country match from the 1st tee of the old course to the 18th green of the new course, about two miles. The low score was 43.

During World War II, some members planted victory gardens on land adjacent to the golf course.

The 1923 fire was the genesis of the Schenectady Curling Club. While the new clubhouse was under construction, the Mohawk curling rink was turned into a locker room. So a new curling club was started.

During the Depression and World War II, Mohawk faced tough times. Membership dropped off, and the club closed on Mondays. The Depression may be responsible for this "tradition," which continues at many private clubs to this day.

After World War II, the character of the club changed from a men's club to a family club. Baby boomers came along and more women started to play golf.

A swimming pool was added in 1953.

Mohawk has an excellent written history. A 70-page bound booklet was produced for their 75th anniversary, and a 130-page hard cover book was published for their centennial. The editors were Roy Stratton and Ned Landon.

NEW COURSE AT ALBANY

ALBANY, NY

Public, 18 holes

	Par	Slope	Rating	Front nine	Back nine	Total
Front tees	71	113	72.0	2306	2684	4990
Middle tees	71	116	68.7	2648	3078	5726
Back tees	71	117	69.4	2848	3331	6179

CHRONOLOGY

1932   The course designed by John Melville and named Albany Municipal Golf Course opens; construction began in 1930. The course is about 4800 yards, par 70. The grand opening foursome is Melville, Mayor John Boyd Thacher, Alfred Schlosser from the Public Works Department and Alfred Sporborg, a City Council member.

1991   The entire course is redesigned by Bob Smith, pro at Wolferts Roost, and Ed Bosse, pro at Colonie Country Club. A driving range is added and a new clubhouse built.

NOTES

During the first year, 1932, almost 30,000 rounds were played. Green fees were 50¢ and season passes were $10.

There is room for expansion at the 300-plus acre course.

There is a cross country ski trail laid out for winter use.

The original layout was so hilly the course could not have golf carts. The back nine was hillier, so almost 90 percent of the rounds were played on the front nine. Carts were introduced with the redesign of the course in 1991.

The course annually hosts the City of Albany Championships and The Mayor's Challenge Cup.

The course is a member of the Audubon Society.

NICK STONER MUNICIPAL GOLF CLUB

CAROGA LAKE, NY

Public, 18 holes

	Par	Slope	Rating	Front nine	Back nine	Total
Front tees	70	115	68.5	2705	2465	5170
Back tees	70	110	68.0	2905	2605	5510

CHRONOLOGY

1925   A six-hole course opens. These holes are carved out of the wilderness in the Adirondacks. The land is donated by Cyrus Durey with the provision that the town build a golf course, park and playgrounds. Tennis courts and a caddy shack are built. Fred Allen is the first pro; Channing Floyd follows him.

1929   The course expands to 18 holes. Durey donates more land on the opposite side of the road, and a second nine is constructed.

NOTABLE PROS

Steve Jennings: 1983-present. PGA Class "A" Professional and superintendent.
Deb Jennings: 1983-present.   PGA Class "A" Professional.

NOTES

Nick Stoner, a local man, was an officer in the American Revolution. He was a pioneer, patriot and soldier who lived from 1761 to 1853.

Deb and Steve Jennings are a wife/husband pro team.

NORMANSIDE COUNTRY CLUB

DELMAR, NY

Private, member owned, 18 holes

	Par	Slope	Rating	Front nine	Back nine	Total
Front tees	72	117	71.8	2801	2665	5466
Middle tees	70	110	68.6	3086	2984	6070
Back tees	70	111	69.1	3196	3138	6334

CHRONOLOGY

1927 The club forms and the course opens. The founder is William A. Glenn, and the designer is William Harries.

1986 The course is redesigned by Geoffrey Cornish, and a master plan for the golf course is created.

NOTABLE PROS

Ralph Montoya: 1970-84. Former Northeastern New York Player of the Year and member of the Northeastern New York PGA Hall of Fame.

Tom DeBerry: 1987-present. PGA Section president, 1991.

NOTES

In 1952, the club hosted the Empire State Open, a PGA tour event.

In 1991, the club hosted the Northeastern New York PGA Stroke Play Championship.

In 1996, the club hosted the New York State Mid-Amateur Championship.

Otsego Golf Club

SPRINGFIELD, NY
Semi-private, 9 holes

	Par	Front nine	Back nine	Total
Front tees	70	2750	2750	5500
Back tees	70	2939	2939	5878

CHRONOLOGY

1894 The club forms and the course and clubhouse are built. The course has 12 holes. Golfers play them, then repeat the first six to make 18. The longest hole is 332 yards in this day of the gutta percha ball when a long drive was about 150 yards. With some revisions, the clubhouse remains the same today.

1907 The course is reduced to nine holes, probably because some holes were too close to the house of Mrs. Alfred Cooper Clarke, the aunt of one of the founders.

1922 The course is redesigned by property owner Jack Ryerson and made longer. Only the 1st hole is basically unchanged. The course is essentially the same today.

1942 The club, private for 48 years, becomes semi-private due to financial conditions brought on by World War II. Non-members pay a daily greens fee.

1968 A not-for-profit corporation is created with Arthur R. H. Clarke as president, Tom Goodyear as vice president and secretary, and Frederick S. Doolittle as treasurer and course manager.

1986 Ryerson dies. His will has a provision that allows Victor Salvatore, Jr. to purchase the 85 acres on which most of the course is situated. If he does not buy it, the land goes to the Episcopal Diocese of Albany. If he buys it, the money goes to the Diocese and the Diocese has the right to set the fair price. Salvatore forms a corporation and sells stock to members and friends. A price of $200,000 is negotiated with the Diocese. Today there are two corporations, one that owns the property and one that runs the golf operation.

NOTABLE PROS

Fitzjohn brothers: Val, Fred and Ned: 1894-01. Val was second in the US Open, 1899.

OUTSTANDING MEMBERS

Charles Sloan: 1921-67. He served as superintendent and is credited with keeping the course going despite difficult times during the Depression and World War II.

NOTES

The prime founders were Henry L. Wardwell and Leslie Pell-Clarke. They were classmates at St. Paul's School in Concord, NH. They owned adjacent estates on which the course was built. Wardwell's estate was called Pinehurst and Pell-Clarke's was called Swanswick. Part of Swanswick is the home of the Glimmerglass Opera House. Pell-Clarke wintered in Orlando, FL where he built a nine-hole course in 1892.

Other founders of the club were George Hyde Clarke, A. Beekman Cox, Henry C. Bowers, John H. Bowers and William Constable. Two years after the course opened, Henry C. Bowers was killed by lightening under a tree on the present 3rd hole. A bronze cross marks the tree.

Pell-Clarke died in 1904. His role as prime supporter of the club was taken over by Arthur Ryerson, who died in the sinking of Titanic in 1912. Five years later, the widow of Pell-Clarke, Henrietta, sold the property to Reyerson's widow, Emily. She was the president from 1933 to 1939 and was followed by her son, Jack, from 1940 to 1967.

Samuel S. Spaulding was president from 1912 until his death in 1933.

Every Labor Day since 1933, the Schwartz family of Cherry Valley has held a golf tournament. They have a tradition of firing a small cannon on the first hole as each group tees off. Otsego believes this tournament is the oldest, continuous family sporting event in the country.

Golfers from Cooperstown used to arrive at the course by steamboat. Steamboat service stopped in 1931.

Pheasant Hollow Golf Club

CASTLETON, NY

Semi-private, 9 holes

	Par	Slope	Rating	Front nine	Back nine	Total
Front tees	74	na	na	3025	3025	6050
Back tees	74	na	na	3315	3315	6630

CHRONOLOGY

1962   The club founded by Peter and Ed Sultan opens. The designer is William Mitchell.

1986   Paul Roth purchases the property.

1992   Joe Bove, a PGA professional, and Fred Kassner, the owner of Liberty Travel, purchase the property.

1991   The clubhouse is completed. The building was originally a farm house built in 1928.

1996   An improvement plan is implemented, and the course is redesigned by Al Zakoris of Cannan, ME.

NOTES

The course was carved out of a meadow and took two years to complete.

Fred Kassner and Joe Bove invested $550,000 to help save and improve the course.

The club plans to add nine holes by 2000.

PINE BROOK GOLF CLUB

GLOVERSVILLE, NY

Private, member owned, 9 holes

	Par	Slope	Rating	Front nine	Back nine	Total
Front tees	72	123	72.5	2754	2757	5511
Back tees	71	120	69.1	2960	3165	6125

CHRONOLOGY

1923   The club forms as the Sir William Johnson Country Club. The founders sell bonds, purchase the 169-acre Simmons farm, convert the farmhouse into a clubhouse and hire James Floyd, a Scottish golf pro, to design a nine-hole course.

1937   The club files bankruptcy due to the Depression. The property is purchased by Samuel Rothschild, Julius and Daniel Higier and Morrell Vrooman as the RHV Realty Corp. A group of golfers forms the Cloversville Golf Club and leases the property from RHV. At the first meeting the name is changed to Pine Brook Golf Club, and Harold Bernard is elected president.

1946   Pine Brook purchases the property from RHV for $10,000.

1997   A new, free standing pro shop is built, the kitchen, dining and lounge area are expanded and the locker rooms are renovated.

NOTABLE PROS

Doug Turnesa: c.1938.   His brothers, Mike and Willie, were nationally recognized golfers. Willie was a US Amateur Champion.

OUTSTANDING MEMBERS

Edward Vonderahe: Member for 60 consecutive years.

NOTES

Tommy Armour, Joe Kirkwood and Babe Didrikson played exhibitions at Pine Brook.

Harold Bell has been at the club since 1979. He operates the restaurant and lounge.

Pine Brook hosts a county Junior Golf Tournament each summer sponsored by the members and a local bank.

PINEHAVEN COUNTRY CLUB

GUILDERLAND, NY

Private, 18 holes

	Par	Slope	Rating	Front nine	Back nine	Total
Front tees	73	122	73.0	2972	2992	5964
Middle tees	71	115	69.3	3082	3098	6180
Back tees	71	117	70.4	3252	3262	6514

CHRONOLOGY

1959   The club forms and the first nine holes designed by Jim Thompson of Mohawk and Armand Farina of Schenectady Municipal open. The Brown farmhouse is used as the clubhouse.

1960   An 18-hole course designed by Thompson and Farina opens in June.

1962   A new clubhouse is built. The Spike Lounge area and fireplace were part of the Brown farmhouse.

1964   A water system is installed. Before the system, there was little grass and a great deal of sand. The size of the putting green is doubled.

1965   A swimming pool and bathhouse are built.

1987   The clubhouse is renovated and the size of the pond by the 17th tee is doubled.

1989   The driving range is improved and expanded. Wider tee areas are created.

1993   The pro shop is damaged by fire and rebuilt at the same location. A cart barn is added.

1996   An automatic irrigation system is installed for tees, greens and fairways. The pond is expanded by one third to bring water into play on the 2nd hole.

1997   The new Spike Lounge, a member's dining room and a locker room for women are built. An elevator is added to the clubhouse.

1998   The 16th hole is redesigned and water now comes into play. The banquet facility and kitchen are remodeled. Meeting, office and storage space is created.

NOTES

The first group to play the course was Jim Thompson and Armand Farina, the designers, with Robert Haggerty of Edison, Hap Duval of Stamford and Steve Savel of Western Turnpike.

In the early days there were 19 holes. The first was was played as a practice hole.

Bob Hope, Mickey Rooney, Englebert Humperdinck, Bill Devane and Mac Davis have played the course.

Pinehaven has hosted the following major tournaments:
        1986 and 1989 – Capital District Open
        1987 – NYS Junior Boy's Championship
        1992 – NYS Ladies Senior Championship
        1998 – NYS Men's Amateur

The club originally had a Board of Directors that represented the stockholders. They also had a Board of Governors that represented the members. This latter Board was disbanded in the 1970s. Currently, the Board of Directors operates the club. All members on the Board are required to be stockholders. Club members may or may not be stockholders. Members serve on a variety of advisory committees.

PIONEER HILLS GOLF CLUB

BALLSTON SPA, NY
Public, 18 holes

	Par	Slope	Rating	Front nine	Back nine	Total
Front tees	70	na	na	2106	2427	4533
Middle tees	70	na	na	2598	2598	5196
Back tees	70	na	na	2728	2694	5422

CHRONOLOGY

1995   The club forms and a nine-hole course opens. The course is owned and operated by Lobo Pioneer, Inc. The founders — Allen Hills Sr., Allen Hills Jr., and Gloria Wheeler – design the course.

1997   A second nine opens.

NOTES

The name, Pioneer Hills, has an interesting origin. Allen Hills Sr. was a State Trooper who wanted to build a golf course. It was a "pioneer" venture for him. Since the land had many hills and his last name was Hills, he put it all together to create the name.

Father and son, Allen Sr. and Jr., conceived Pioneer Hills in 1990. The project was delayed and even shut down due to federal wetlands concerns. At one point, the land was seized by the US Government.

The course is heavily wooded, has several water holes and is built on rolling land. The intended look is that of an "Augusta North."

PLEASANTVIEW GOLF CLUB

FREEHOLD, NY

Semi-private, 9 holes

	Par	Slope	Rating	Front nine	Back nine	Total
Front tees	74	118	70.0	2883	2883	5733
Middle tees	72	122	70.4	3250	3250	6500
Back tees	72	124	71.3	3363	3363	6726

CHRONOLOGY

1968   The club is founded by Eugene Schmollinger.

1969   The course designed by Francis Duane opens; a water system is installed.

1992   The property is purchased by Ron Herron.

1995   Bill Gressick draws the design for another nine probably opening in 2000.

1997   Final grading, fairways seeded and tees are built for new holes 10, 11 and 12.

1998   Final grading for new holes 13-16 is completed.

NOTABLE PROS

Bill Gressick: 1968-83.   Lifetime member and past national officer of the PGA.

OUTSTANDING MEMBERS

Mr. & Mrs. Mike Fandozzi: 1969-97. Both have been club champions several times. Continuous members since 1969.

NOTES

Bill Gressick is consultant to the pro shop manager and he acts as tournament director.

The golf course is part of a resort that has 92 rooms and a restaurant serving breakfast and lunch.

QUEENSBURY COUNTRY CLUB

LAKE GEORGE, NY

Public, 18 holes

	Par	Slope	Rating	Front nine	Back nine	Total
Front tees	70	106	66.5	2487	2268	4755
Middle tees	70	105	64.7	2836	2700	5536
Back tees	70	112	67.4	3081	2986	6067

CHRONOLOGY

1955   The club forms and a nine-hole course opens. The founders are Mark Cassidy and Glenn Shattuck. Cassidy, who holds a degree in landscape architecture from Cornell University, designs the course.

1959   Nine holes designed by Cassidy are added.

1965   Shattuck sells his half of the operation to Norman Canavan. Mark Cassidy Jr. is given his father's share.

1969   A new clubhouse is built after the original clubhouse, a renovated barn, burns down.

1970   Eugene Smith replaces Canavan as half owner.

1976   Eugene and "Cissy" Blanche Smith buy out Mark Cassidy Jr.

1985   Scot Smith, their son, becomes a partner. A graduate of the Stockbridge Farm School, he is the current superintendent. Scot installed the first water system for the tees and greens.

NOTABLE PROS

"Putt" Bernard Lamay: 1984-present

OUTSTANDING MEMBERS

Betty Cornell: 1954-present
"Red" Mervin Male: 1969-84

NOTES

The Betty Cornell Invitational has been held every September since 1960. Betty Cornell was a physical education teacher who played a major role in the history of the club. The tournament is held in September, but is sold out by May. It attracts women golfers from Connecticut, Massachusetts and Vermont as well as New York.

The Men's Fall Invitational has been played each year since 1964. In 1983, it was renamed the "Red" Male Invitational. Red was a member and friend who helped the Smiths make a success of the golf course. Over 30 of his friends from Ogdensburg play in the tournament each year. Red died in 1984.

Mark Cassidy Sr. was very popular, and many members followed him to Queensbury from another club. In the early 50s, he would often pay employees in stock when he was short of money, then buy the stock back – a delayed paycheck.

The club has a putting green and a driving range with three instructors.

The course is in a beautiful Adirondack setting and has more than 50 perennial flower beds.

The clubhouse serves lunch and has a bar. Banquet facilities can handle up to 144 people. Outdoor steak roasts can serve 250 people.

Rainbow Golf Club

GREENVILLE, NY

Semi-private, 18 holes

	Par	Slope*	Rating*	Front nine	Back nine	Total
Front tees	71	na	68.0	2320	2024	4344
Middle tees	71	119	69.2	3145	2647	5792
Back tees	71	na	na	3391	2853	6244

*Course was in transition from 9 to 18 holes and all figures were not available at time of publication.

CHRONOLOGY

1917-39 The site of Birmann's Farm, a 300-cow dairy farm that takes in boarders for a dollar a day.

1939-76 As the resort business booms, the farm is phased out and is replaced by Rainbow Lodge Resort. More rooms and recreational facilities are added.

1956 A five-hole golf course opens. Walter Birmann Sr. and Jr. are the founders. The course is designed by Walter Sr.

1957 Two more holes are added.

1958 Two more holes are built, bringing the total to nine.

1968-76 The original nine is renovated to accommodate a new nine.

1976 Walter Jr. and Carl Birmann purchase the property from their father and form two corporations. Rainbow Lodge operates the restaurant/motel and Rainbow Golf Club and Resort operates the club.

1976-96 A second nine designed by Walter Birmann, Jr. is added.

NOTABLE PROS

Walter Birmann is a Class "A" PGA Professional and the only pro in the history of the club.

NOTES

Otto and Anna Birmann came from Switzerland and Germany in 1903 to Hillside, NJ. For health reasons they moved to Greenville and purchased the 300-acre farm. Development of the New York State Thruway hurt the resort business and the golf course was added.

When the new holes were added in 1958, one was a par 5 that was shared with Rainbow Airport, a grass strip. The scorecard advised players to stand aside when planes took off or landed.

Two holes, the 12th and 13th, have an island green and a seven-acre lake that comes into play. They are called "double trouble."

Facilities include a driving range and a golf school as well as full resort amenities.

RIP VAN WINKLE COUNTRY CLUB

PALENVILLE, NY

Public, 9 holes

	Par	Slope	Rating	Front nine	Back nine	Total
Front tees	72	118	70.1	2698	2652	5350
Back tees	72	115	68.5	3005	3001	6006

CHRONOLOGY

1919   The course is designed by Donald Ross.

1920   The course opens.

1941   The course closes due to World War II.

1949   Raymond and Patricia Smith of New York City, who had a summer home
in Palenville, purchase the property.

1950   The course reopens.

NOTES

The course is open from April to November. It is surrounded by mountains with
breathtaking fall colors. There are doglegs, water holes, and the third is a Donald
Ross signature hole. Each hole has a name, often related to Rip Van Winkle.

RIVERVIEW COUNTRY CLUB

REXFORD, NY

Public, 18 holes

	Par	Slope	Rating	Front nine	Back nine	Total
Front tees	74	124	73.4	2536	2482	5018
Middle tees	73	120	70.7	3370	3120	6490
Back tees	73	128	73.7	3675	3420	7095

CHRONOLOGY

1966   The club forms as the Walhalla Country Club and the course designed by William Mitchell opens.

Sacandaga Golf Club

NORTHVILLE, NY

Semi-private, 9 holes

	Par	Slope	Rating	Front nine	Back nine	Total
Front tees	73	116	68.4	2561	2594	5155
Back tees	72	118	68.2	3012	2995	6007

CHRONOLOGY

1898   The club forms and a four-hole course opens. The course is owned by the Fonda, Johnstown and Gloversville Railroad.

1903   The course expands to nine holes designed by a Mr. Sherman. The clubhouse is built and also serves as the main office for the railroad.

1952   The railroad goes bankrupt and the 750-acre property is sold to a Florida group headed by Edward Noulin.

1953   Brothers Bill and Sparakus Delia purchase the course from the Florida group.

1954-56 The course is leased to Stan Cruz.

1955   Everett and Herbert Singer buy the golf course.

1980   The Singers sell the course to PGA professional Pat Palmieri.

1985   PGA professional and life member Richard Osborne purchases the property and is the current owner.

NOTABLE PROS

Channing Floyd: 1920s-1933.   First pro of note and recognized as a fine teacher.

Frank McGuinness: 1933-36, 1968-73. Continued to teach golf until he was almost 90.

Robert Ray: 1936-42.   Started the Sacandaga Open that attracted top PGA
                              pros. The tournament was played until the early
                              1950's.

Lionel F. Callaway: 1942.   He was the creator of the Callaway Handicap System.

Gene Kunes: 1951.   Winner of the Canadian Open.

Billy Gormley: 1993-present. PGA Class "A" Professional and the general
                              manager of the club.

OUTSTANDING MEMBERS

Bob Venner: 1933-64.   Served as shop assistant under Frank McGuinness and as
                       caddie master. From 1964 to 1980, he was the full-time
                       superintendent of the golf course.

NOTES

Sacandaga was the first golf club in Fulton County. It celebrated its centennial in
1998. Sacandaga is an Indian word meaning "land of the waving grass." The
original pro shop is still being used. The third hole, a 220-yard par 3, is the only
one of the original four holes in play today.

The course record for nine holes was set in August, 1940 by Bob Venner who shot
29, including an eagle on the 287 yard 9th with a drive and a two-foot putt. It was
tied in August, 1994 by Casey Russom. The 18- hole record was set on Aug. 20,
1960 by Fiske Warren who shot 31/32 = 63.

In 1959, Doris and Bob Venner won the ladies' and men's club championship
respectively. It was believed to be the first time among area clubs that a husband
and wife won in the same year.

In the early 1900s, Velma Venner worked for the railroad and collected greens
fees: $1 for the day. Arthur Venner, her husband, was one of some 70 caddies.
Caddie fees were 15¢ plus tip for nine holes. Sacandaga Park was attracting up to
5,000 visitors per weekend. Transportation was provided by the railroad. The Park
was called the "gem of the Adirondacks" and the golf course was referred to as
"Sacandaga's superb golf links." Arthur and Velma were the parents of Bob
Venner.

Sagamore Resort and Golf Club

BOLTON LANDING, NY

Resort, 18 holes

	Par	Slope	Rating	Front nine	Back nine	Total
Front tees	70	122	73.0	2710	2501	5211
Middle tees	70	128	71.5	3222	3188	6410
Back tees	70	130	72.9	3395	3414	6809

CHRONOLOGY

1928   Donald Ross designs the course and it is built under his personal supervision. The course is located on Federal Hill, about one mile from the hotel that was built in 1882.

1929   The course opens.

1979   The hotel and course close.

1983   A partnership of Kennington Properties of Los Angeles and Norman Wolgin of Philadelphia purchases the property from Louis Brant.

1985   The course reopens. It is restored according to Ross's original blueprints. A $56 million investment is made in the property, and the project is on-going.

NOTES

Donald Ross brought heather from his native Scotland to highlight the course.

The Sagamore, a four-star resort on its own 72 acre island in Lake George, has been awarded the Silver Medal by Golf Magazine. Trillium, named for the flower, is its signature restaurant. The resort has a 17,000 square-foot conference center that can host small seminars to large banquets.

Ross had a policy of not making the first hole facing east, to avoid the morning sun. However, the view on Federal Hill was so beautiful to the east that he violated the rule for this course.

Ross's daughter, who is in her 80s, visited the course in 1997. She remembered the construction of the course from when she was a teenager.

Sagamore has a driving range, practice putting green and fully equipped pro shop. Lessons are available. Tom Smack has been the Director of Golf and head professional since 1984.

 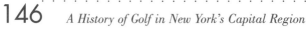

Saratoga Golf And Polo Club

SARATOGA SPRINGS, NY

Private, 9 holes

	Par	Slope	Rating	Front nine	Back nine	Total
Front tees	73	118	71.6	2744	2743	5487
Back tees	70	112	68.8	3046	3027	6073

CHRONOLOGY

1896   The club is organized on 75 acres owned by James M. Andrews and called the Saratoga Golf Club. The farmhouse is converted into a clubhouse. J.S. Mott, a civil engineer, produced a map of the course.

1931   The name is changed to Saratoga Golf and Polo Club. The Saratoga Golf Club Real Estate Corporation purchases 43 of the 75 acres.

1953   The club purchases 29 acres along Seward Street from from the Putnam family.

1956   The club purchases 12 acres from William H. Moran, Inc. along Church Street.

1961   Part of the Denton Farm is purchased.

1968   The club purchases six acres along Church Street and two acres along Plank Street from Peter Issaris. This includes the former Ostrander home that Ostrander called Hylands. Issaris operates the Dorian restaurant out of the home. The club converts the building into a clubhouse.

1995   The clubhouse is updated.

NOTES

In 1937, the heart of the Depression, the club faced difficult financial times. Thirteen members stepped forward to provide funds that saved the club. They formed the Little Club Owners, Inc. and took over the deed. The deed was returned to the club in 1949. A plaque in the clubhouse honors these 13.

When the course was opened in 1896 there were four practice holes ranging in length from 100 to 250 yards.

Saratoga Spa Executive Course

SARATOGA SPRINGS, NY

Public, State owned, 9 holes

	Par	Front nine	Back nine	Total
Front tees	58	1605	1605	3210
Back tees	58	1635	1635	3270

CHRONOLOGY

1964　　The course opens.

NOTABLE PROS

Tom Creavy: 1963-74.

John Taylor: 1975-95.

Jack Polanski: 1975-95.

Saratoga Spa Golf Course

SARATOGA SPRINGS, NY

Public, State owned, 18 holes

	Par	Slope	Rating	Front nine	Back nine	Total
Front tees	72	122	72.0	2817	2794	5611
Middle tees	72	125	70.0	3257	3102	6359
Back tees	72	130	74.0	3580	3498	7078

CHRONOLOGY

1963   The course designed by William Mitchell opens.

1988   A new pro shop is built.

1990   A water system is installed.

NOTABLE PROS

Tom Creavy: 1963-74.
John Taylor: 1975-95.
Jack Polanski: 1975-95.

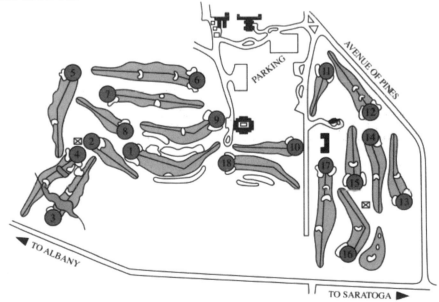

SCHENECTADY MUNICIPAL GOLF COURSE

SCHENECTADY, NY

Public, city owned, 18 holes

	Par	Slope	Rating	Front nine	Back nine	Total
Front tees	72	115	68.1	2600	2675	5275
Middle tees	72	118	69.4	3080	3175	6255
Back tees	72	123	71.1	3225	3345	6570

CHRONOLOGY

1935   The club forms and the course designed by Jim Thompson, Mohawk Golf Club pro, opens. It is a joint venture of the City of Schenectady and the Federal WPA program.

NOTABLE PROS

Tony Pacelli: 1935-53.
Armand Farina: 1954-66.
Bob Haggery: 1967-present.

NOTES

The course hosts the Gazette Amateurs: Seniors, Men and Women as well as the Schenectady Two Man Best Ball.

In 1997, the Northeastern New York Championship was held at the course.

Schuyler Meadows Club

LOUDONVILLE, NY

Private, 18 holes

	Par	Slope	Rating	Front nine	Back nine	Total
Front tees	72	127	72.5	2986	2587	5573
Middle tees	72	126	71.9	3532	3035	6567
Back tees	72	129	73.2	3645	3142	6787

CHRONOLOGY

1926   The club forms and work on the clubhouse and golf course starts. The property had been known as the Hartman Farm.

1927   The course designed by Devereux Emmet opens. The clubhouse designed by Albany Architect J. Worthington Palmer is completed. He used George Washington's Mount Vernon as a model. The contractor is John B. Waldbillig & Co.

1983   A long-range plan for the course is developed by the architectural firm of Cornish and Silva.

1989   The clubhouse is expanded to create the McCahill Room and a new kitchen. The expansion is designed by the Wagoner and Reynolds. The contractor is Barry, Bette and Led Duke.

1990   Architect Geoffrey Cornish updates the long-range plan and discusses a practice range.

NOTES

The club was formed by a group of Loudonville men who belonged to Albany Country Club, located on Western Avenue. They felt that was too far away and wanted a location that was more convenient.

The first president was John A. Manning.

The Meadows has hosted the Sarazen Scholarship Tournament every year since its inception in 1982. The Scholarships, named for Gene and Mary, are awarded to 16 Siena College students each year, four from each class. Approximately 180 golfers play each year. About $40,000 is raised annually and the fund now has an endowment of more than $1 million. Dr. Sarazen has an honorary degree from Siena.

SHAKER RIDGE COUNTRY CLUB

ALBANY, NY

Private, member owned, 18 holes

	Par	Slope	Rating	Front nine	Back nine	Total
Front tees	72	123	72.0	2976	2575	5551
Middle tees	71	121	70.4	3316	3043	6359
Back tees	71	124	72.2	3472	3286	6758

CHRONOLOGY

1929　The club forms and the course designed by Joseph A. Field and James K. Thompson, the pro at the Mohawk Club, opens. The site was the 300-acre Leonard Bol Dairy Farm. It was called the North Shaker Farm, after the North family of the Shaker sect who had lived there for several generations. The club leases the property with an option to buy. The farmhouse is remodeled into a clubhouse. Joseph A. Field is the first president.

1932　On Dec. 28, three days before the scheduled New Year's Eve party, the clubhouse burns down.

1942　The back nine closes due to the loss of younger members who went into military service in World War II.

1945　The back nine is redesigned and reopens. A major addition is made to the clubhouse, providing more space for the locker room, kitchen and dining room.

1948　A swimming pool is added, perhaps the first at a local country club.

NOTABLE PROS

Hap Duval: 1948-49.

George Ramsden: 1950-75.

Charles W. Conrad: 1976-present.

NOTES

Joseph A. Field, a member of the Colonie Country Club, sponsored some friends for membership in that club. They were rejected, so he started Shaker Ridge.

Shaker hosted the Capital District Skins Game for several years. This charity benefit involves four tour pros each year. In the past Arnold Palmer, Lee Trevino, John Daly, Fuzzy Zoeller, Scott Hoch, Chi Chi Rodriguez, Ed Fiori and Blaine McCallister have played.

In the 1993 Skins Game, John Daly attempted to drive the green of the 326 yard, par 4, 11th hole. His first drive ended up in the water. He reloaded, hit the ball 12 feet from the hole, and made the putt for a par.

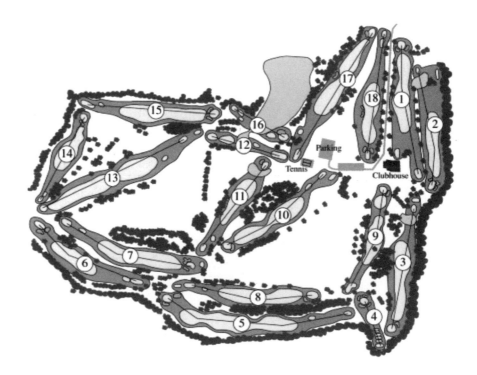

SKENE VALLEY COUNTRY CLUB

WHITEHALL, NY

Semi-private, 18 holes

	Par	Slope	Rating	Front nine	Back nine	Total
Front tees	73	117	71.8	2995	2693	5688
Middle tees	72	116	70.3	3285	3170	6455
Back tees	72	121	71.8	3535	3288	6823

CHRONOLOGY

1967   The club forms and a nine-hole course designed by Mark Cassidy opens. The founders are Clifford and Patricia Sparks. A water system for the tees and greens is installed. A barn is converted into the clubhouse.

1991   Cassidy does a rough layout and a second nine is added. Cliff Sparks finishes the design and builds the course. A water system is installed for the tees and greens.

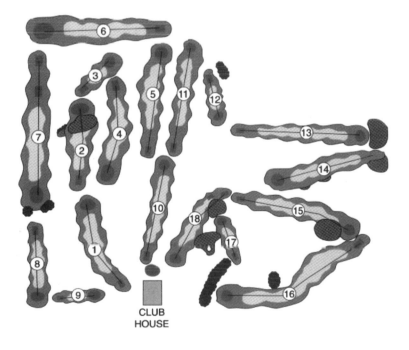

STADIUM GOLF CLUB

SCHENECTADY, NY

Public, 18 holes

	Par	Slope	Rating	Front nine	Back nine	Total
Front tees	71	106	68.5	2810	2613	5423
Middle tees	71	110	67.7	3110	2849	5959
Back tees	71	113	69.5	3291	3025	6316

CHRONOLOGY

1957   The club forms and a nine-hole course opens at the site of the Schenectady Baseball Stadium. The founder, Peter McNearney, is the owner of the Schenectady Blue Jays. These nine holes are outside the stadium. The team folds after 1957, and a pitch and putt course is built inside the stadium.

1965   Edmund and Stefanie Hennel and Henry and Wanda Lewkowicz purchase the club. Edmund and Wanda are brother and sister. These families own land adjacent to the stadium.

1970   The pitch and putt course closes and a driving range opens in its place.

1983   A new pro shop is added to the clubhouse.

1987   The original nine is redesigned and a new nine is added. The designer is Douglas Hennel. Only two of the original holes remain; these are replaced later, so that none of the original holes now exist.

1995   An automated irrigation system is installed for the entire course.

NOTABLE PROS

Leo Callahan: 1966-71. Aided the new owners in the operation of the club.

NOTES

Peter McNearney was a beer distributor and bottler in Schenectady. The baseball stadium sometimes was called McNearney Stadium.

The original nine holes were private, but the pitch and putt course was public. The public had the impression that the stadium was a pitch and putt course.

Edmund Hennel and Henry Lewkowicz operated the club from 1966-72. In 1972, Roger Hennel became the manager. He died in 1997. Doug Hennel became the president. Gregory Hennel is the course superintendent.

The driving range has grass tees and its own irrigation system.

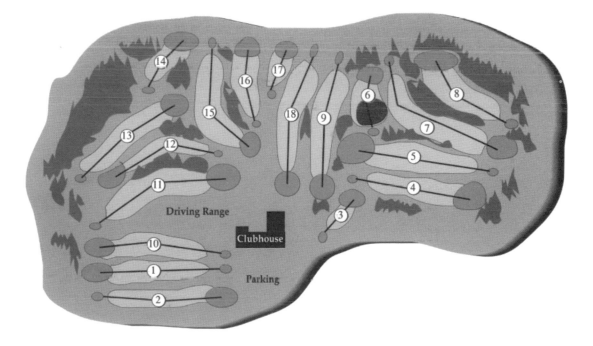

SUNNY HILL RESORT AND GOLF COURSE

GREENVILLE, NY

Public, 18 hole executive course

	Par	Front nine	Back nine	Total
Tees	66	1700	2650	4350

CHRONOLOGY

1920   Peter and Gurine Nicholsen of Norway and Brooklyn purchase a 110-acre farm and the resort opens.

1968   The first nine holes designed by Nicholsen, the son of Peter and Gurine, open. The course is 1700 yards, par 30. A new clubhouse is built and a water system for tees and greens installed.

1988   The second nine designed by Arnold Nicholsen and Hal Purdy opens. A water system for tees and greens is installed.

NOTES

The name Sunny Hill comes from the fact that even when it is cloudy in surrounding areas, the sun often shines on the hill.

In Colonial times, the property was known as the Edgett Farm.

In 1968, more than 4000 rounds were played on the 1700-yard course and only two equaled or broke par.

The resort has a putting green and a driving net. There are no sand traps on the course.

The resort has 100 rooms and many recreational facilities.

Sunnyside Golf Course

QUEENSBURY,NY

Public, par 3, 9 holes

	Par	Front nine	Back nine	Total
Tees	54	870	870	1740

CHRONOLOGY

1959   The course opens after being built and designed by Robert Scherer out of an apple orchard. The clubhouse is a converted 8' x 10' foot chicken coop. The course has lights for night play.

1965   A new clubhouse and bar are constructed.

1967   Hal Purdy redesigns the course.

1970   Lights are removed.

1977   The Jacobs family purchases the property.

1978   A dining room is added to the clubhouse.

1990   An irrigation system is installed.

NOTES

When the course opened, the greens fee was 75¢ for the day.

An evening league of 40 golfers, started in the 1960s, still exists.

The course is well shaded, has one dogleg and one water hole with a partial island green.

SYCAMORE COUNTRY CLUB

RAVENA, NY
Public, 18 holes

	Par	Slope	Rating	Front nine	Back nine	Total
Front tees	72	114	70.7	2705	2902	5607
Middle tees	71	113	68.8	2953	3194	6147
Back tees	71	115	70.1	3187	3341	6528

CHRONOLOGY

1971   The club forms and the course designed by Frances Duane opens. The Bill Weis family is the founder.

1991   The property is sold to Joe Bove, a PGA professional, and Fred Kessner, owner of Liberty Travel.

NOTABLE PROS

Barry Vavrineck: 1971-94.

OUTSTANDING MEMBERS

Billie Armstrong: Ladies Club champion for eight years and Senior Ladies champion for seven years.

Bruce Roberts: Seven-time club champion.

NOTES

On the right side of the 5th fairway stands the largest Sycamore tree in New York State as measured by the Department of Forestry.

The clubhouse is a converted barn that was built in 1871. It is 80' high and 210' long. It is made of oak and uses wooden pegs instead of nails. There is a full service bar and restaurant.

TACONIC GOLF CLUB

WILLIAMSTOWN, MA

Semi-private, 18 holes

	Par	Slope	Rating	Front nine	Back nine	Total
Front tees	71	123	69.9	2447	2755	5202
Middle tees	71	121	68.9	2833	3169	6002
Back tees	71	127	71.7	3150	3490	6640

CHRONOLOGY

1896   The club forms as the Taconic Club and a seven-hole course opens. The founders and designers are William H. Doughty, James M. Ide and Edward C. Gale, all of Troy. They are joined by Henry N. Sabin and James Bullock. The first clubhouse is a small building owned by Bullock off Main Street.

1912   The second clubhouse is the Whitney Sampson House on South Street.

1926   The course is redesigned by Stiles and Van Kleek.

1927   Through the generosity of some alumni and friends, Williams College becomes the owner of the 100-acre site. The course had been situated on 150 acres. Fifty of the acres had been leased. The heirs of the owners want the land for their use, and the course is redesigned.

1928   The club incorporates and is run separately from Williams College. The course is converted to an 18-hole, par 73. Pro Richard Baxter supervises this modification.

1955   Par is changed to 71. Again, Baxter supervises the conversion.

1956   The present clubhouse is constructed.

1995-6 A complete water system is installed.

NOTABLE PROS

Richard Baxter: 1924-63.   Also served as the greens superintendent, planted many of the trees and supervised the development of the course.

Rudy Goff: 1963-83.

Rick Pohle: 1983-present.

NOTES

Taconic has hosted the following tournaments:

    1956   US Junior Amateur Championship.

    1958   NCAA Championship. (Combined University and College)

    1963   US Women's Amateur Championship.

    1972   NCAA Championship. (College only)

    1992   Massachusetts State Open.

    1996   US Senior Amateur Championship.

Jack Nicklaus aced the 14th hole in 1956 at the age of 16.

Dick Chapman, Williams '34, won the US, British, French and Canadian Amateur Championships.

Bing Crosby and Gene Sarazen played the course in 1956.

Many of the leading pros have played the course, including Al Geiberger, Tommy Aaron, Phil Rodgers, Deane Beman, Joanne Carner and Dottie Pepper.

George Shultz Jr., former Secretary of State, is an honorary member and frequently plays the course.

The course record from the back tees is 67 and is held by Richard Tworig, Tommy Aaron, Lloyd Monroe, Wayne Pence, Andy Morse and Ed Kirby. Rick Pohle holds the record from the middle tees, a 64 (twice). Mary Gale has the women's record, 72.

The Boston Globe rated Taconic the seventh most difficult and fourth most pleasurable to play of the 200 best courses in the Northeast.

TEE-BIRD COUNTRY CLUB

FORT EDWARD, NY

Public, 18 holes

	Par	Slope	Rating	Front nine	Back nine	Total
Front tees	70	106	68.5	2609	2626	5235
Back tees	70	106	68.7	3056	3108	6164

CHRONOLOGY

1960   The club forms.

1962   A nine-hole course opens. Bruce and Jean Irwin are the founders, and
Bruce designs the course.

1980   A second nine is added. Daniel Irwin is the designer.

NOTABLE PROS

Bruce Irwin: He was a Class "A" PGA Professional for 30 years until his death
in 1986.

NOTES

Same owners as the Tee-Bird South Course.

Patty Berg attended the ceremonies that marked the opening of the second nine in
1980.

TEE-BIRD SOUTH COURSE

FORT EDWARD, NY

Public, 9 holes

	Par	Slope	Rating	Front nine	Back nine	Total
Front tees	68	na	na	2275	2275	4550
Back tees	68	na	na	2656	2960	5616

CHRONOLOGY

1993   The club forms and the nine-hole course opens.

NOTES

Same owners at the Tee-Bird Country Club.

The course has a driving range and the Tin Fox Restaurant.

THOUSAND ACRES GOLF CLUB

STONY CREEK, NY

Public, 9 holes

	Par	Slope	Rating	Front nine	Back nine	Total
Front tees	70	na	na	2569	2569	5138
Back tees	70	107	67.4	2829	2865	5694

CHRONOLOGY

1970   Construction begins for a course designed by owner Jack Arehart, Joe
        Hanlon and George Doherty. The builder is Don Baker.

1971   The course opens.

1996   New front tees are added.

NOTABLE PROS

Joe Hanlon: 1971-93.
Franz Feigenwinter: 1994-96.
Matt Bruce: 1997-present.

NOTES

The name is derived from the fact that the entire resort covers 1000 acres. There
is horseback riding as well as other activities.

The course is in the third generation of Arehart family management. Patrick
Arehart is the general manager of the resort. His brother, Jeremy, manages the golf
course.

The course is very scenic. Four of the holes play along the Hudson River and
water comes into play on every hole. The greens are very fast and considered
excellent.

The course record for nine holes is 29 by a Virginia amateur.

TOP OF THE WORLD GOLF RESORT

LAKE GEORGE, NY

Public, 9 holes

	Par	Slope	Rating	Front nine	Back nine	Total
Front tees	72	101	66.5	2321	2321	4642
Middle tees	72	107	67.2	2770	2770	5540
Back tees	72	110	67.9	2868	2868	5736

CHRONOLOGY

1939   The course opens informally as part of a resort. The founder is Charles Tuttle of New York City. Hendrix Van Rensselaer, who is the superintendent of farms for Tuttle, designs and builds the golf course.

c.1942   The course closes due to the war.

1948   The course reopens on a formal basis and is made available to the public.

1982   Property is sold by Tuttle's son, Croswell, and town homes are developed.

1991   Property is leased from the Galesi Group by the Feeney family.

NOTES

The property was purchased by Charles Tuttle in 1926. It was a chicken farm.

Many of the old buildings have been restored recently and consideration is being given to expanding the golf course.

TOWN OF COLONIE GOLF COURSE

COLONIE, NY
Public, 27 holes

	Par	Slope	Rating	White nine	Blue nine	Total
Front tees	72	113	71.4	2895	2915	5810
Middle tees	72	129	70.1	3180	3190	6370
Back tees	72	132	72.5	3420	3425	6845

CHRONOLOGY

1967   The Town Board approves more than $1 million for a golf course project. Town Board member Saul Greenhouse is the major force behind the project and Town Supervisor William Sanford is a key supporter. The 199 acres are purchased from Glenn Roberts, Ralph Bruno, Wellington Kugler and Edward Scharfenberg.

1968   The clubhouse is built.

1969   An 18-hole course opens. It is designed by William Mitchell, who also worked on the Saratoga Spa Course. An irrigation system is installed.

1982   Nine additional holes designed by Robert Trent Jones open. An irrigation system is installed.

1998   Another nine holes, these designed by Rick Jacobson, who formerly worked with Jack Nicklaus, are opened.

NOTABLE PROS

Tom Gunning: 1975-present.   Class "A" PGA professional. He has two sons, Jay and Jeff, who are fine golfers and work with him in the pro shop. Jay won the State Amateur Championship in 1986.

NOTES

The White to Blue nines are considered the tournament course.

The course has hosted the Futures Tournament since 1983.

James G. Zambardino, superintendent of Parks & Recreation, has worked with the course since it opened in 1967.

The philosophy has always been to create a course of championship quality with regard to length and skill for all the nines.

At present, more than 70,000 rounds are played per year. With the new nine, annual rounds should top 100,000. The revenue has always covered debt service and operating costs.

With the new nine, the course will go to 36 holes. The sequence of play will be Red to White, White to Blue, Blue to Green and Green to Red. The White to Blue will still be considered the tournament course.

VAN PATTEN GOLF COURSE

JONESVILLE, NY
Public, 27 holes

	Par	Slope	Rating	White nine	Red nine	Total
Front tees	72	113	70.1	2675	2840	5515
Middle tees	73	117	69.0	3055	3184	6239
Back tees	73	121	71.1	3285	3355	6640

CHRONOLOGY

1969   The club forms and an 18-hole course designed by Armand Farina opens. Robert Van Patten Sr. is the founder. A water system is installed.

1970   A third nine, also designed by Farina, is added.

NOTABLE PROS

Armand Farina: 1969-76.
Al Caferelli: 1976-85.
Dave Lewis: 1998.

NOTES

Van Patten has three nines. The White/Red (shown above) are used for major tournaments. The other combinations are as follows:

	Red/Blue nines	Blue/White nines
Front tees	115/70.7	112/69.3
Middle tees	116/69.6	110/69.0
Back tees	120/71.5	116/70.8

A one-day North Atlantic professional tournament was held in 1998.

Van Patten sponsors an Annual Cancer Day Tournament.

VAN SCHAICK ISLAND COUNTRY CLUB

COHOES, NY

Private, member owned, 9 holes

	Par	Slope	Rating	Front nine	Back nine	Total
Front tees	73	117	71.1	2710	2705	5415
Back tees	72	115	71.3	3224	3232	6456

CHRONOLOGY

1895 The club forms and two holes are constructed. The 1st hole is located on the site of the present 6th hole. The 2nd is where the present 1st is located.

1900 The club incorporates as the Island Golf Club. The first clubhouse, which had been an abandoned barn, burns down.

1901 An acre of land is purchased from the owners of the Van Schaick Mansion in order to build a new clubhouse. Today's clubhouse is on the same site, though it has been altered, modernized and expanded several times.

1906 Cohoes Savings forecloses on the mortgage. Arvin W. Harrington buys the property from the bank for $18,150 and forms Van Schaick Realty Company. The intent is to develop the land. Some lots are sold, but the golf course is expanded.

1915 The course expands to nine holes designed by Jack Gormley.

1916 The Realty Company changes the name to Van Schaick Island Country Club.

1930 A water system is installed.

1936 A fire destroys most of the clubhouse.

1937 The clubhouse is rebuilt with a new lounge, ladies' locker room and fireplace. The men's locker room is moved upstairs and expanded.

1948   The course adds more and larger tees so the length can be extended and varied to make a more interesting second round.

1958   Membership reaches 155.

1965   The clubhouse undergoes major renovations. A new irrigation system is installed. Membership reaches 225 and is closed at that number.

NOTABLE PROS
John Gaucas: 1949-74.
Bill Dupuis: 1975-81.
Stew Smith: 1982-present.

NOTES
The Algonquin Indians occupied the island when Henry Hudson arrived in 1609. In 1665, Captain Goosen G. Van Schaick and Phillip Pieterse Schuyler purchased the island for one bushel of wheat. They called it Havers Island. In 1674, Van Schaick bought out Schuyler. In 1767, the island was called Peebles and Oat Island. By 1823, the name was changed to Van Schaick Island and Little Platt. Around 1852, the name was changed to Adam Island. The name was changed back to Van Schaick at the turn of the century.

The Van Schaick Mansion was built in 1735 and is occupied today. It is the last known original building on the island.

At one time there was a race track in the area of the 1st and 2nd holes. Members owned harness horses.

Since there were few automobiles in the early years, members came by horse and buggy, trolley car, bicycle and boat. Many walked a long distance.

Wedgewood Golf Club

GREENWICH, NY

Public, Par 3, 9 holes

	Par	Red nine	Blue nine	Total
Tees	54	550	725	1275

CHRONOLOGY

1974   The course and clubhouse open. The course is designed by Mike Evanico Sr., whose family builds and owns it. No substantial changes have been made to the course.

NOTES

Three holes run along the Champlain Canal.

The clubhouse has a full service bar, but serves no food. Golf outings and banquets can be arranged.

The course hosts five leagues each week.

WESTERN TURNPIKE GOLF COURSE

GUILDERLAND, NY

Semi-private, 27 holes

	Par	Slope	Rating	Red nine	Blue nine	Total
Front tees	36	117	69.0	2628	2509	5137
Middle tees	36	124	68.6	3191	2835	6026
Back tees	36	127	70.6	3396	2970	6366

CHRONOLOGY

1930   The club forms as the Realty Golf Corp. The principals are Ed Vrooman and John Veeder.

1932   An 18-hole course designed by Jim Thompson, pro at the Mohawk Golf Club, opens.

1942-47 The course is closed due to World War II.

1950   An irrigation system is partly installed.

1963   The course is modified and expanded to 27 holes.

1965   Automatic water on tees/greens and manual operations on the fairways are installed.

1986   The clubhouse burns down.

1987   A new clubhouse is built on the same site.

1988   A putting course is constructed.

NOTABLE PROS
William Rapp: 1932-36.
Armand Farina: 1937-42.
John Gaucas: 1947.
Steve Savel: 1948-79.
Herb Moreland: 1980-97.

OUTSTANDING MEMBERS
Al Huba

NOTES
Western has three nines. The figures above are for the Red and Blue nines which have the highest slope figure of any combination from the back tees. The other combinations are as follows:

	Red/White nines	White/Blue nines
Front tees	68.7/118	68.1/118
Middle tees	69.1/123	67.3/120
Back tees	71.3/126	68.9/123

The Szatkowski family has been involved with the club from the beginning. Amelia Szatkowski married Ed Vrooman in 1930. Ed died in 1941 and the club closed. Amelia's brother, Steve Szatkowski reopened the club after the war. Art Szatkowski [Satoski] became the owner 1962 when his brother, Steve, died.

None of the original holes still exist. Satoski has been the designer for the modifications and the new holes.

The course covers more than 300 acres of land. More than 50,000, 18-hole rounds are played each year. The club serves the public, has members and leagues. For golf outings, more than 300 players can be accommodated in a day.

The clubhouse has a full service restaurant/bar and banquet facilities for wedding receptions and other events.

WHISPERING PINES GOLF CLUB

SCHENECTADY, NY

Public, 18 hole executive course

	Par	Front nine	Back nine	Total
Front tees	55	1100	910	2010
Back tees	55	1240	1075	2315

CHRONOLOGY

1965   The club forms and a nine-hole course opens. The founder is Burnham B. Armstrong, who designs the course with Phil Mitchell. An irrigation system is installed.

1968   A second nine opens, also designed by Armstrong and Mitchell.

1985   The property is purchased by Burnham's three sons, Kirk, Mark and Brett.

1990   A driving range opens.

NOTABLE PROS

Kirk Armstrong: 1972-present. Class "A" PGA pro.

OUTSTANDING MEMBERS

Ed Febbie: Original course record holder with a 50. He has had 28 holes in one in his career.

NOTES

The range has a practice bunker and chipping green.

The course is excellent for beginners and for practicing the short game.

The target time for playing 18 holes is two hours and 20 minutes.

Windham Country Club

WINDHAM, NY

Semi-private, 18 holes

	Par	Slope	Rating	Front nine	Back nine	Total
Front tees	72	114	68.4	2335	2541	4876
Middle tees	71	123	68.1	2565	3135	5700
Back tees	71	127	69.9	2788	3300	6088

CHRONOLOGY

1927   The club forms.

1928   A nine-hole course designed by architect Len Rayner of Cooperstown opens.

1966   A second nine designed by Hal Purdy opens. A water system is installed for fairways and greens.

1990   An automatic irrigation system is installed for fairways, tees and greens.

1997   An additional 90 acres of land adjacent to club property is purchased, possibly for use as a driving range.

NOTABLE PROS

Dave Rarich: 1981-present.   Class "A" PGA Professional. He wrote a booklet, "How   to Beat the Windham Golf Course."

OUTSTANDING MEMBERS

Hon. Clarence D. Lane, member of the State Assembly.

NOTES

The club is owned by 94 stockholders.

The club hosts an Annual Amputee Golf Scramble and an Annual American Cancer Society Tournament.

Windham also hosts the State Trooper Open and the Fireman's Open.

The time course record for 18 holes is one hour and 29 1/2 minutes.

Joe Gerlak served as pro prior to World War II. When he went into the service, his brother, Alex, took over. When Joe returned from the service he became the pro again.

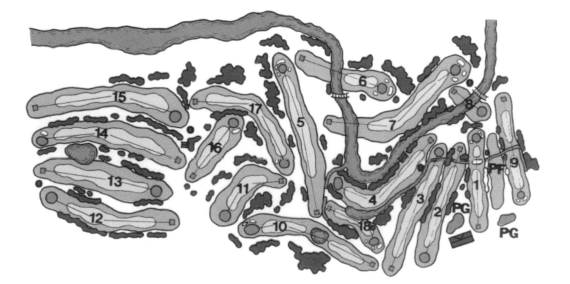

WINDING BROOK COUNTRY CLUB

VALATIE, NY

Semi-private, 18 holes

	Par	Slope	Rating	Front nine	Back nine	Total
Front tees	73	121	72.4	2916	2949	5865
Middle tees	72	107	66.9	3135	3179	6314
Back tees	72	110	68.2	3310	3304	6614

CHRONOLOGY

1962   The club forms and an 18-hole course designed by the club founder, Paul J. Roth, opens. The clubhouse opens, also.

1963   An underground irrigation system is installed.

NOTABLE PROS

Claude Young: 1962-68.

George Lauretti: 1969-76.

James Rothenberg: 1977-present. Rothenberg is a Class "A" PGA Professional who has written several articles for PGA Magazine and Golf Journal. The theme of his articles is "what takes place in the golf swing if done exquisitely."

NOTES

The club name comes from the brook that winds its way through both nines.

Winding Brook opened with 390 members in 1962. There are still 27 active charter members.

After World War II, there was a nine-hole course at the present site of Winding Brook. There was also a restaurant called the White Horse Inn. The restaurant burned down in the 1950's and the course closed. Some people called this course Silver Brook.

Arnold Palmer played the course in 1965 and 1967.

Bob Golby and Ken Venturi played in 1969.

Winding Brook hosted the New York State Junior and Boy's Championship in 1980.

Al Austin, the grandson of founder Paul Roth, is active in the management of the club.

The club dining room is open to the public and has banquet facilities.

WINDY HILLS GOLF COURSE

GREENWICH, NY

Public, 9 holes

	Par	Slope	Rating	Yards
Red tees	34	112	33.7	2425
White tees	34	109	32.5	2605
Blue tees	34	111	32.8	2677

CHRONOLOGY

1994   Joe Kehn, who owns the course with his wife, Karen, designs and constructs the course on 200 acres. They bring in 500 loads of loam and lay six miles of underground wire and pipe. The course has a full irrigation system. The greens are Southshore bent grass from Loft's. The fairways are blue grass.

1995   The course opens.

1998   The clubhouse opens.

NOTES

Nine new holes are planned for the fall of 1998. The present nine has three par 3s and one par 5. The new nine will have two par 5s and one par 3. The yardage for the new nine will be 3300. Total yardage will be about 6000.

The deck on the roof of the clubhouse provides scenic views of Vermont and the Adirondacks. The Greenhouse restaurant serves a light menu and beer/wine.

WOLFERTS ROOST COUNTRY CLUB

ALBANY, NY

Private, member owned, 18 holes

	Par	Slope	Rating	Front nine	Back nine	Total
Front tees	70	120	70.6	2737	2500	5237
Middle tees	70	124	69.3	2926	2937	5863
Back tees	70	128	71.1	3152	3103	6255

CHRONOLOGY

1886   The Albany Press Club, a social club located in downtown Albany, opens. The first clubhouse is at 28 North Pearl St. They move to 25 Beaver St. and then to 106 State St.

1907   Membership grows to over 150 and the name is changed to City Club of Albany.

1915   Membership is now 390, and they purchase about 50 acres to build a golf course. The name is changed to Wolferts Roost, Inc. The majority of the land was the estate of the late Gov. David B. Hill who had died in 1910. The property was vacant. Gov. Hill names the property after a book by Washington Irving: *Wolferts Roost and Other Tales*. Hill had purchased the land from Joseph Kline Emmet, a very successful actor. The original nine holes are laid out by Harold Andrews, an Albany civil engineer and amateur golfer. They have sand greens. The grand opening of the course is on Sept. 11, 1915. George Dow, the pro at the Island Club of Troy, plays an exhibition.

1916   Fifty acres are purchased from the Van Rensselaer estate.

1921   A. W. Tillinghast is hired to redesign the original nine holes and add nine more. The greens are changed to grass during this transition.

1924   The new course opens on July 23 with an exhibition by Walter Hagen.

1926   On November 13, the clubhouse, the original mansion, is destroyed by fire.

1927   A new clubhouse is built on the same site.

1931   Forty more acres are purchased and the course is redesigned. The architect is Leonard Ranier of Cooperstown.

1938   The course is redesigned again, and this is essentially the present course. During the late 1930's, some land along Loudonville Road is sold for residential development due to financial problems stemming from the Depression.

1964   An automatic water system is installed.

1968   A new field house is constructed to replace the carriage house and stable that had been renovated in 1915 for the men's locker room.

1989   A new addition to the clubhouse is completed.

NOTABLE PROS
Jerry Dwyer: 1917-33.
Jack Gormley: 1934-57.
Bob Smith: 1957-91. Served as assistant to Jack Gormley from 1953-57.
James Tureskis: 1992-present.

OUTSTANDING MEMBERS
Elmer F. DeTiere: President from 1930-47.

NOTES
In the early years, resident members had to live within 20 miles of Albany City Hall. Dues for a resident member were $40 per year; family members paid another $10. If you wanted to play golf, you had to pay $5 more for a season pass. A guest green fee was 50¢ a day, $2.50 per week and $7 for a month.